ICT and It's Applications in Agriculture

About the Editors

Golla Ravi is assistant professor in School of Agriculture, MBU University. He has completed M.Sc. Agriculture from Professor Jayashankar Telangana state Agricultural University and Ph.D. from Central Agricultural University Meghalaya. He has cleared ARS NET (2021&2023) and UGC NET (2021&2022). He also the author of 6 research papers and 4 book chapters and participated in different conference, trainings and workshops.

Md. Mubeena is assistant professor in S.V.Agricultural College, Tirupati. She worked as SMS in KVK Banavasi, Kurnool. Research Associate III in Centre for Agribusiness Incubation, ICAR-NRCM, Hyderabad. She has completed M.Sc ag. and Ph.D in Agricultural Extension from Acharya N.G. Ranga Agricultural University. She has cleared ARS NET (2018). She is also the author of 10 research papers and 8 book chapters and participated in different conference, trainings and workshops.

Apoorva Veldandi is a Ph.D. Research Scholar in the ICAR-National Dairy Research Institute, Karnal. She has completed M.Sc. and B.Sc. Agriculture from Professor Jayashankar Telangana State Agricultural University. She has cleared ARS-NET (2023) and UGC-NET(2022). She is also the author of 3 research papers, 1 review paper and 8 book chapters and participated in different conferences, workshops and seminars.

Pallavi Shaktawat, a dedicated research scholar is currently pursuing Doctoral research in the Department of Agricultural Extension, School of Social Science, College of post graduate studies in agricultural sciences, CAU-I, Umiam, Meghalaya. She holds a B.Sc. (Agriculture) Degree from SKRAU, Bikaner in 2021. Continuing her academic journey, she joined M.Sc. in Agricultural Extension from CPGS-AS, CAU, Imphal (Manipur) in 2023. So far she contributed Two research papers in NAAS rated National Journals, Two book chapters, one AESA meeting note and Three popular articles. She has also participated in different conference, trainings and workshops.

ICT and It's Applications in Agriculture

Golla Ravi
Agricultural Extension
School of Social Sciences
College of Post Graduate Studies in Agricultural Sciences, Umaim
Central Agricultural University
Imphal, Manipur

Md. Mubeena
Agricultural Extension
S.V. Agriculture College
Acharya N.G. Ranga Agricultural University
Tirupathi, Andhra Pradesh

Apoorva Veldandi
Agricultural Extension
Division of Dairy extension
National Dairy Research Institute
Karnal, Haryana

Pallavi Shaktawat
Agricultural Extension
School of Social Sciences
College of Post Graduate Studies in Agricultural Aciences, Umaim
Central Agricultural University
Imphal, Manipur

PMW

PMW
FU 75, Pitam Pura
New Delhi 110034
publishmywork23@gmail.com
Mob. 91-8447075807

ISBN: 978-93-61341-82-3

Preface

In today's rapidly advancing technological landscape, the integration of Information and Communication Technology (ICT) has significantly transformed various sectors, including agriculture. This comprehensive overview delves into the profound impact of ICT and its applications within the realm of Indian agriculture. Exploring the evolution and implementation of technology in farming practices, this study sheds light on the innovative tools and strategies revolutionizing the way agricultural processes are conducted, managed, and optimized. Through this insightful exploration, we aim to understand the pivotal role of ICT in empowering farmers, enhancing productivity, and fostering sustainable agricultural practices across India.

Contents

1

ICT Technologies in Agriculture

Golla Ravi

Agricultural Extension, School of Social Sciences
College of Post Graduate Studies in Agricultural Sciences, Umaim
Central Agricultural University-Imphal 793103

Information and communication technology (ICT) is the combination of hardware, software and the means of production that enables the collection, exchange, processing and management of information and knowledge. It includes social media, portals, websites, kisan call centers and expert systems *etc.,*

Need of ICT in agriculture and rural development

- For increasing the productivity and efficiency in agriculture
- Globalization, Modernization, Challenges and Opportunities across the world for Sharing of knowledge.
- Public Expenditure and gaps in extension could be reduced
- For effective utilization of available platforms
- Penetration of smartphones even in villages and the transfer of information

Role of ICT in agriculture

- Integration of digital technologies in agriculture generates extensive big data, valuable for improved policymaking and monitoring.
- ICT serves as a cost-effective bridge between farmers, researchers, and extension agents, facilitating collaboration and information sharing.
- Market information services enabled by ICTs grant farmers access to nearby markets and insights into consumer demands.
- ICTs foster networking among agricultural stakeholders, enhancing market access for inputs, product marketing, and trade.

- Real-time, actionable information provided by ICTs aids governments and farming communities in disaster prevention and management.
- ICT trends hold promise for driving sustainability in agriculture, enhancing efficiency, transparency, and traceability.
- ICTs empower rural and smallholder farmers by improving access to financial services, affordable insurance schemes, and risk management tools.
- These technologies serve as crucial educational tools, broadening opportunities for women, youth, and other beneficiaries, thereby enhancing livelihoods and incomes.
- Budget-friendly mobile phones, internet access, and related services disseminate climate-smart solutions and knowledge for effective implementation.

Information and communication technologies (ICT) are diverse set of technological tools and resources used to transmit, store, create, share or exchange information. These technological tools and resources include computers, the Internet (websites, blogs and emails), live broadcasting technologies (Radio, Television and Webcasting), recorded broadcasting technologies (podcasting, audio and video players, and storage devices) and telephony (fixed or mobile, satellite, visual/videoconferencing, etc.). Tools of Information and communication:

1. Computer

An electronic device for storing and processing data, typically in binary form, according to instructions given to it in a variable program.

Generation of computers

First Generation (1946-1959)

- Vacuum Tubes & Valves for logic circuitry
- Input Punch cards & paper tapes.
- Output-Magnetic tapes.
- Programming Language: Machine code Vacuum Tubes were invented by Sir John Ambrose Fleming
- Examples: UNIVAC, EDVAC, EDSAC, ENLAC, IBM-701, IBM-650

Second Generation (1959-1965)

- Transistors
- Transistors were invented by-William Shockley, Walter Brattain & John Bardeen.
- Batch processing, Multiprogramming 05. Programming Language-Assembly language & high-level programming languages such
- FORTRAN, COBOL, etc.
- Examples: IBM 7000, CDC 1604, ATLAS, NCR 304.

Third Generation (1965-1971)

- Integrated Circuits
- Integrated Circuits were invented by Jack Kilby.
- Remote processing, time sharing, multiprogramming OS.
- Programming Language FORTRAN (II-IV), COBOL, PASCAL PL/1, BASIC ALGOL-68, etc.
- Examples-IBM 360/370, Honeywell 6000 series, PDP (Personal Data Processor).

Fourth Generation (1971-1980)

- VISI (Very Large Scale Integrated) Microprocessor circuits.
- Tune-sharing, real-time networks, distributed OS.
- Programming Language-C, C++, DBASE, etc.
- Examples- DEC 10, STAR 1000, PDP 11, CRAY 1(Super Computer), CRAY X-MP (Super Computer).

5. Fifth Generation (1980 onwards)

- ULSI (Ultra Large-Scale Integration) Microprocessor circuits.
- Parallel Processing & Artificial Intelligence technology
- Programming Language C and C++, Java, .Net, etc.

2. Radio

The radio refers to the wireless transmission and reception of electromagnetic signals, typically in the form of radio waves. Radios play a crucial role in telecommunications, broadcasting, and wireless networking, enabling the transmission of audio, data, and other information over long distances without the need for physical connections.

The radio came from a series of discoveries and inventions in the late 1800s and early 1900s. The first contributor, the one responsible for opening the door to all radio, is Heinrich hertz.

Role of radio in agriculture and rural development

Radio plays a crucial role in agriculture and rural development, especially in areas where access to other forms of communication or technology might be limited.

- **Information Dissemination:** Provides vital data on agriculture, weather, prices, policies, and best practices.
- **Education and Training:** Educates farmers on new technologies, crop methods, pest control, and livestock management.
- **Community Engagement:** Encourages participation through discussions, Q&A sessions, and shared experiences.
- **Market Access:** Facilitates informed decisions on selling produce, finding buyers, and fair pricing.
- **Extension Services:** Connects farmers with expert advice, consultations, and guidance.

Limitations of radio in agriculture and rural development

- **Reach and Accessibility:** Weak signals in remote areas limit access.
- **Illiteracy & Language Barriers:** Limits understanding for those with limited literacy or different languages.
- **Tech Advancements:** Struggles to keep up with more interactive digital communication methods.
- **Limited Interactivity:** Lacks real-time interaction, making individual queries challenging.
- **Reliance on Infrastructure:** Depends on consistent electricity and infrastructure, challenging in some areas.

While radio remains an essential tool for agricultural and rural development, its effectiveness can be limited by various factors. Integrating it with newer communication technologies and considering local needs and limitations can help maximize its impact in these contexts.

2. Television

Television (TV) comes from the Greek word (tele), meaning "distant" or "far," and the Latin visio, meaning "sight" or "vision." It is a mode of (tele) communication typically used for transmitting moving (color) images (and potentially sound) to audiences. From around the 1950s onward, television increasingly became the primary medium in the Western world for shaping public opinion because of the saturation of television in society.

Television in India had its inception in 1959 when the first terrestrial broadcast was launched in Delhi. TV was only available on the state-run Doordarshan network up until the early 1990s. The advent of satellite television in the late 1990s led to a television boom, with hundreds of channels offering diverse content.

Role of Television in agriculture and rural development

- **Visual Learning:** Offers visual demonstrations, enhancing understanding compared to radio or print media.
- **Education and Extension:** Disseminates modern methods, technologies, policies, and best practices widely.
- **Market Information:** Provides market insights aiding informed decision-making for farmers.
- **Entertainment-Education:** Engages and educates through entertaining agricultural content.
- **Awareness and Advocacy:** Raises awareness, advocates for farmers' rights, and showcases success stories.

Limitations of Television in agriculture and rural development

- **Access & Infrastructure:** Relies on electricity, infrastructure, and equipment, inaccessible in remote or disadvantaged areas.
- **Cost & Production:** Creating quality content is expensive, maintaining equipment adds financial strain.
- **Language & Literacy:** Language barriers and literacy levels can limit effectiveness.
- **Limited Interactivity:** Offers limited real-time interaction, lacks immediate viewer engagement.
- **Competition with Other Content:** Faces competition for viewership, impacting reach and impact.

While television has the advantage of visual communication and a broader reach compared to radio, it also faces challenges related to infrastructure, production costs, and engagement limitations. Integrating television with interactive technologies or combining it with other communication channels might help overcome some of these limitations, enhancing its role in agricultural and rural development.

3. Mobile

The first functioning cell system and first real cell phone call in 1973 was developed by Martin Cooper of Motorola. The first commercial service began in 1983 with the advent of the legendary Motorola DynaTAC 8000X. In 1983 the world's first transportable mobile phone was called the Motorola DynaTAC 8000X.

4. Internet

During the 1960s, the internet originated as a project initiated by the United States Department of Defense, aiming to build a decentralized network. This initiative, known as ARPANET (Advanced Research Projects Agency Network), was developed by the Pentagon's Advanced Research Projects Agency in 1969. It was intended to establish a secure and resilient communication network for entities involved in defense-related research.

The technology behind electronic message transmission, known as Internet Protocol (IP), was formulated during this period. IP governed the packaging, addressing, and transmission of electronic messages across the network. The creation of TCP/IP (Transmission Control Protocol/Internet Protocol) in 1977 standardized this protocol. TCP/IP facilitated the direct linking of diverse networks to ARPANET, which eventually evolved into what is now recognized as the Internet.

As the network expanded, researchers and professionals from various disciplines began utilizing it. Eventually, the National Science Foundation (NSF), having developed a similar network named NSFNET in parallel, adopted much of the TCP/IP technology from ARPANET. This led to the establishment of a distributed network of interconnected networks capable of handling substantial traffic.

In 1985, NSF initiated a program to extend Internet accessibility across the United States. They established a backbone infrastructure called the NSFNET, opening access to educational institutions, academic researchers, government agencies, and international research bodies. By the 1990s, the Internet witnessed rapid expansion, with estimates suggesting a doubling of connected computers annually.

Advantages of the Internet

- Internet revolutionized banking with e-banking platforms.
- E-commerce websites offer convenience for shopping.
- The Internet serves as a source of social media platforms like Facebook, Instagram, and Twitter connect people globally.
- Education transformed with online classes accessible to students worldwide.
- Information Access: Provides extensive agricultural knowledge, market prices, and weather forecasts.
- E-Learning: Offers online courses and tutorials for skill development.
- Market Access: Facilitates direct selling, expanding customer reach.
- Precision Agriculture: Enables optimized resource use and crop monitoring.
- Networking: Connects farmers globally for collaboration and advice.

Limitations

- Access and Connectivity: Limited internet availability in rural areas.
- Digital Divide: Socioeconomic disparities impact access and skills.
- Cost and Infrastructure: Expense in setting up and maintaining internet infrastructure.
- Content Relevance: Lack of localized or pertinent information.
- Reliability: Dependence on electricity for internet access.

5. Newspaper

A printed publication (usually issued daily or weekly) consisting of folded unstapled sheets and containing news, articles, advertisements, and correspondence. A newspaper is a periodical publication containing written information about current events.

Role and limitations of radio in agriculture and rural development

- **Information Dissemination**: Provides updates on farming techniques, market prices, weather forecasts.
- **Policy Awareness:** Informs farmers about government policies, subsidies, and agricultural schemes.

- **Education:** Educates farmers about modern practices and solutions to farming challenges.
- **Market Access:** Offers a platform for advertising produce and discovering market opportunities.
- **Community Building:** Fosters a sense of community among local farmers.

Limitations of radio in agriculture and rural development

- **Limited Reach:** Restricted access in remote or underdeveloped areas.
- **Timeliness:** May not always offer up-to-date information, especially on rapidly changing aspects.
- **Language/Literacy Barriers:** Tailored to specific languages or literacy levels.
- **Cost and Accessibility:** Purchasing might be expensive for some rural populations.
- **Depth of Information:** Space constraints limit in-depth coverage of agricultural topics.

While newspapers are valuable for disseminating information, their limitations include reach, timeliness, language barriers, cost, and depth of content. These factors can hinder their effectiveness in rural development.

2

Cyber Extension

Nazreenbanu Tahasildar

Department of Agricultural Extension Education
University of Agricultural Sciences, Raichur

Cyber extension

Cyber extension means extension over cyberspace. In the applied context of agriculture cyber extension means using of power of online networks, communications channels and interactive multimedia to improve information access for farmers, extension workers, research scientists and extension managers.

Advantages of cyber extension

1. Cyber extension will save time, money, and effort
2. Cyber extension reduces the dependence of the farmers on extension functionaries
3. Easily accessible in remote areas
4. Can provide an early warning system before the natural disaster
5. Cyber extension will be available continuously.

Limitations of cyber extension

1. Cyber extension is becoming a tool for development communication. However, most rural communities are not yet able to take advantage of this new tool due to illiteracy, lack of skills and economic power.
2. It cut steps from the extension process like training and zonal workshops.
3. There will be both irrelevant and relevant messages, not all messages will be suitable for all farmers.
4. Cyber extension establishment requires high investment.

Cyber Extension is an important mechanism to support the Extension functionaries and bridges the communication gap between the four pillars of the Extension system- The Research, Extension, Marketing and Farmers.

1. To expand knowledge resource
2. To accelerate agricultural growth
3. To facilitate better information access
4. To supplement inadequate technical manpower
5. For stronger Research – Extension – Client system linkage
6. To develop an efficient feedback mechanism
7. For cost-effective extension delivery
8. To develop knowledge managers
9. To ensure gender equity in the technology transfer process
10. To empower small and marginal farmers
11. To serve the farm stakeholders beyond the technology transfer role

Application of Cyber extension

Websites and Portals: Online platforms offering a wealth of agricultural information, resources, news, and interactive features for farmers.

Mobile Applications: Apps providing farmers with on-the-go access to weather forecasts, market prices, pest identification, crop management tips, and expert advice.

Social Media Platforms: Utilizing platforms like Facebook, Twitter, WhatsApp, and YouTube to share agricultural content, facilitate discussions, and connect farmers for knowledge exchange.

E-learning Platforms: Online courses, webinars, and tutorials tailored to agricultural topics, allowing farmers to learn at their own pace and convenience.

Interactive Decision Support Systems: Software and tools that analyze farm data, offering insights and recommendations for optimized crop management, irrigation, and pest control.

Remote Sensing and GIS Tools: Using satellite imagery and geographic information systems to monitor crop health, soil conditions, and land use, aiding in precision agriculture.

Teleconsultation Services: Video conferencing, chat, or helpline services connecting farmers with agricultural experts for real-time advice and consultations.

Precision Agriculture Technologies: Implementing IoT devices, sensors, drones, and automated systems for precise monitoring and management of crops, soil, and livestock.

Online Marketplaces: Platforms enabling farmers to sell their produce directly to consumers or access larger markets without intermediaries.

Data Analytics and Big Data Solutions: Analyzing large datasets to derive insights for better decision-making in farming practices and resource management.

Changing role of Extension agent

1950s to 1960s (CDP era): Focusing mainly on organized effort in rural reconstruction, instrument to transform social and economic life of rural people, Transfer of technology i.e. confined only to High Yielding varieties of cereals.

1960s to 1970s: Target area extension (DPAP, DDP) and Target group approach (SFAL, SFDA).

Mid 1970s: T&V extension system: linear Transfer of Technology/Top to down technology transfer or top -down policy formulation under single line of technical and administrative command.

1980s to 1990s: extension focus on providing self Employment/wage employment to rural areas, community asset creation (TRYSEM, JRY).

1990s to 2000s : Decentralized bottom up ToT through ATMA and ATIC.

2000s (ICT era): extension focus on strong potential of ICT to improve the efficacy and efficiency of the agricultural extension system & digitize the whole agricultural research knowledge and make it available to farmers at their door step in best possible way.

Constraints faced by the farmers in the adoption of ICT platforms in agriculture

1. Technological constraints

- Lack of availability of content in local language
- Too many steps to get information.
- Problems in the maintenance of ICT platforms

2. Economic constraints

- High cost of internet connection.
- Purchasing cost of mobile

3. Social constraints

- Lack of acceptability for internet information.
- Lack of institutional support from the extension and research fraternity
- Less networking among farmers community

4. Psychological constraints

- Lack of motivation
- Lack of interest
- Techno-phobia

5. Personal problems

- Low level of education
- low annual income of the farmers
- lack of awareness on ICT platforms
- lack of knowledge on utilization of ICT platforms.

Ways to forward for better adoption of ICT platforms by the farmers

- Conducting more awareness programs on ICT platforms on marketing and weather platforms etc.
- Developing information and communication technology (ICT) policies for agriculture and rural development.
- Funding for ICT research and development for the benefit of farmers in the budget
- Farmers, researchers, and extension employees in SAUs, as well as officers from agriculture departments, receive regular training in the use of ICTs.
- Follow up mechanism should be included after the introduction of ICT platforms.
- Updating the Knowledge, skills regarding the use of Tech-enabled Platforms

- Provisions should be made for subsidies in internet subscriptions and phone recharge to always increase affordability for farmers to seek information on agricultural activites.
- Network fluctuations and erratic power supplies should be decreased through the development of necessary infrastructure to better serve rural farmer.

3

Conference and Webinars

Asodi Yamini Leela

Department of Agricultural Extension Education, Agricultural College
Acharya N. G. Ranga Agricultural University, Bapatla

Conference

A conference is a formal gathering where people come together to discuss, exchange ideas, present research and engage in discussions on specific topics or fields of interest. These gatherings can vary widely in scale, purpose and format, bringing together professionals, researchers, academics, industry experts, or enthusiasts.

Audio conferencing

Its also called Teleconference, which means meeting a group or party via a phone call instead of meeting them physically. In most cases, standard telephone lines and speakerphones are employed. The person who starts the audio conference called the calling party and the people who are attending the calls are known as participants. Technology requirement of the audio conference:

1. Phone/Computer with access to internet connection
2. Speakers
3. Microphone

Advantages

1. The equipment required to set up an audio conference is simple and less expensive.
2. Options for selecting telephone or speakerphones and networks are many.
3. Audio conferences can be easily recorded by the students themselves for reference.
4. Distant students can also participate in the conference from anywhere.

Disadvantages

1. Difficult to explain abstract concepts in an audio conference due to lack of visual information.
2. Scheduling is necessary and needs coordination between teacher availability.
3. Since eye contact is not possible it is difficult to retain the attention of students.

Video conferencing

Videoconference (also known as video teleconference) is a set of interactive telecommunication technologies which allow two more locations to interact in a two-way video and audio transmissions simultaneously. It is a remote meeting between two or more individuals present in geographically dispersed locations. Users can meet and share information virtually from wherever they are using videoconferencing equipment and communicate using any network available with them.

Advantages

1. A live conversation between two partners from different locations is possible with the visibility.
2. The experts (scientists) can have virtual contact with the farmers and solve the field problems.
3. Useful in giving training sessions for guest lectures.
4. Useful in monitoring the progress of various activities.
5. Reduces the cost of travel and time.
6. Researchers collaborate with colleagues at other institutions on a regular basis without loss of time due to travel.
7. Problem-solving information can be exchanged, and procedural tasks can be discussed.
8. Follow-up for earlier meetings can be done with relative ease and little expense.

Disadvantages

1. Technical failures.
2. Impersonal.

3. Acoustical problems with conference rooms.
4. Greater participant preparation and preparation time are needed.
5. Lack of participant familiarity with the equipment.

Web conference

Web conferencing is any type of online meeting that involves two or more participants in different locations. With a reliable internet connection and conferencing software, they can see, talk, and hear each other in real-time. Web conferencing allows for the sharing of web-based content and is often used as an umbrella term for different types of meeting solutions. Video conferencing is one of these solutions. As the name suggests, it's the technology that enables the sharing of video (and audio) in real-time.

Forms of Web conferencing

1. **Webinars:** This is a term used to describe seminars held online. In webinars, presenters can have document sharing options, while also giving webinar attendees the opportunity to comment or ask questions.
2. **Webcast:** It is a type of online conference that is comparable to a TV broadcast. In this case, there is little or no interaction between the presenter and the conference participants.
3. **Web Meeting:** Web meetings are virtual meetings that encourage interaction among the participants. They include collaboration tools like sharing documents, photos or videos and chat tools.
4. **Online Collaboration:** If only text messages are exchanged, it can mean it's a real-time audio communications conference, but it can also be enhanced with real-time video meetings. Participants can view shared files in order to collaborate on modifications that can be done in real-time during the online collaboration. For example, this gives remote access to remote employees to work efficiently on team projects.
5. **Online Presentations:** Slideshows, Power Point presentations, streaming audio or video and chat functions are used for online presentations. However, for participants to view these presentations they must log in to the online meeting and then they are allowed to interact with the presenter to.

Webinars

Webinars are seminar which are broadcast over the web. These web-based seminars normally required advanced registration to gain permission to access the content and allow for two-way communication, usually in the form of text messages. Like webcasts, webinars can be viewed by single users on one computer screen or by multiple users by connecting the computer to a projector.

When expanded, the webinar definition can be put as "an **online seminar**, workshop or lecture where the speaker(s) deliver presentations and share information to large audiences." A webinar, just like its offline counterpart, is a live event with a specified date and time of occurrence. It allows for the easy presentations of slideshows and documents that would generally be done during a face-to-face gathering. Webinars come under the category of web conferencing – a general term encompassing various other online conferencing methods.

Features of Webinar

Here are some of the basic features of webinars commonly available throughout different webinar software and services –

- Real-time audio, video and text-based communication
- Easy presentation of slideshows, documents and screen content
- Sharing, downloading and recording of complete lectures and sharing or viewing them afterwards.
- Surveys, polls, MCQs, exams, and quizzes

Webinars help presenters interact with their audiences using various elements such as chats, surveys, polls, quizzes, and questionnaires. Attendees can also share the webinar event using social media sites for others to join. If you show up late to a seminar, you miss a portion of it. But there are different types of webinars, some of which help mitigate this issue.

Types of Webinars

Webinars can be classified into three types based on the release and availability of content –

1. **Live Webinars**: Webinars are usually one-time events that occur during a specified date and time. There are no options for scrubbing or pausing a webinar. It goes on just as it would in a seminar taken by a person. Show up late, and you miss a portion of the webinar.
2. **On-Demand Webinars:** Considered a great marketing tool, on-demand webinars allow audiences who have signed up to view it later on at the

time of their liking. Based on the features of the webinar software used, it can even allow for the usage of interactive elements such as polls and quizzes to be used by the viewer.

3. **Automated Webinars:** Automated webinars work in an orderly fashion
   - The presenter records and uploads the webinar to the platform.
   - The date and time of release are set.
   - The webinar is streamed live to the audience when the specified date and time arrive.

Advantages

- Webinars are online, so are easy and convenient to both presenters and participants, as no one has to travel to get to the meeting.
- No type of special equipment is needed, the presenter just broadcasts with a webcam to the participants. Can be set up with very little notice.
- Less cost because it is based on the number of people who sign up.
- Any invitations and registration forms are simple for participants to fill-in online. No need to use the mail so these are less likely to be late or non-existent.
- It is possible for an unlimited amount of audience to attend since it is online.
- It can be recorded so that other people can view in if they can't attend the webinar.

Disadvantages

- Internet speed must be adequate to allow participants to view the presentation without distortion or lag time.
- Audio may be limited to the presenter doing a voiceover and participants can't interact directly.
- If audio is allowed, participants or presenters may have to pay for phone charges.
- No communication is possible through body language if no video feed is available.
- A webinar may not work with all kinds of Internet browsers.
- May not work on Mac computers or mobile devices. This is critical

these days as mobile devices such as tablets, smart phones, etc. are very popular and used widely.

- Other types of technical problems could also occur with the result being the anger and frustration of paying participants, i.e. business firewalls, slow Internet speeds, system configurations incompatible, etc.
- Audience environment may be subject to interruptions or disruptions such as side conversations, having to do other work at the same time, etc.

Web standards

Web Standards is defined as a formal set of standards and technical specifications used to define aspects of the world wide web. These are best-practice standards used by organizations to build web sites and web applications. Web Standards are defined as technologies that are used in building websites. Web Standards consist of technical documents known as specifications, which provide detailed information on how web technology should work.

Web Standards are rules and guidelines established by the World Wide Web Consortium (W3C) developed to promote consistency in the design code which makes a web page. It's simply the guidelines for the mark-up language which determines how a web page.

History

- The main organization credited for setting and maintaining the web standards goes to World Wide Web Consortium (W3C)
- In 1994, World Wide Web Consortium also known as W3C was founded by Tim Berners-Lee.
- With the rise in number of internet user and the various devices used to access the web, hence there came a need to advocate for standards to be set while developing websites. These standards would ensure that the websites work smoothly on all devices even if these contained different configurations
- W3C organization collaborated with many different IT organizations to work on making the standards/governing rules for web development.
- The World Wide Web Consortium publishes set of standards, mostly technical web standards (HTML, CSS, file formats and JavaScript), privacy standards and accessibility standards which also includes different languages that are used in making websites like HTML, CSS, JavaScript, etc. They are not focused on the actual design of websites.

Features of World Wide Web Consortium (W3C)

1. **Web for All:** The basic objective of (W3C) is to make web services available to everyone, regardless of their software or hardware setup or where they reside. This function makes it easier for people all around the world to connect and converse.

2. **Web on Everything:** Because people use a wide range of devices and interfaces, such as mobile phones, tablets, smart assistants, etc., this feature makes sure that every device can readily access the internet.

3. **Web Of Easy Interaction:** Websites should be easy to load and must be interactive so that users don't feel bored. It should be constructed with users' interests in mind.

4. **The Web of Trust:** In order for the web to be secure and to earn the trust of its users, recommendations are made to employ a variety of security measures, such as HTTPS protocol, which is more secure than HTTP, SSL certificates for websites, and many more steps that lessen the danger of attacks on these websites.

Storyboard

A storyboard is a graphic representation of how your video will unfold, shot by shot. It's made up of several squares with illustrations or pictures representing each shot, with notes about what's going on in the scene and what's being said in the script during that shot.

The benefits of storyboarding

A visual aid makes it much easier to share and explain one's vision of the video with others. With a storyboard, it can be shown exactly how the video is going to be mapped out and what it will look like. This makes it infinitely easier for other people to understand.

The video storyboard is a starting point or suggested through line around which you can plan your coverage (all the angles you will shoot of a scene). This really comes in handy when making a video, as it ensures no scenes are forgotten and helps in piecing together the video according to the vision defined.

It might take little while to put the storyboard together however in the long run, it will save time in revision.

Hand-drawn storyboards

The classic storyboarding process is drawing by hand. Just sketching out the scenes for shooting the videos. As mentioned, individual does not need to be a great artist to create a storyboard—stick figures are enough. **The principal goal is to convey the main action that is happening in the shot**, so each frame doesn't need to be very detailed.

Live streaming

Live streaming involves broadcasting video content in real-time over the internet. It allows people to watch events, performances, or activities as they happen, without a significant delay. This technology has become popular across various fields, including gaming, entertainment, education, business, and social media.

Platforms like Twitch, YouTube, Facebook Live, and others enable individuals and organizations to share live video content with an audience. Live streaming has diversified into various niches, such as gaming streams, educational tutorials, live events coverage, Q&A sessions, product launches, and even everyday activities.

The main steps that take place behind the scenes in a live stream

Absolutely, live streaming involves several steps that happen behind the scenes to ensure a seamless broadcast. Here's a breakdown:

Content Creation/Preparation: This is where the content for the stream is prepared, whether it's a presentation, performance, or discussion. Equipment, scripts, or outlines are prepared, and any required media or visuals are readied.

Capture/Input: Cameras, microphones, and any other relevant equipment are set up for capturing the content. This could involve multiple cameras, audio sources, or screen capturing software.

Encoding: The raw audio and video data are converted into a digital format suitable for streaming. This process compresses the data for efficient transmission over the internet.

Transmission: The encoded data is sent to a server. This can be done through an encoder software or hardware that connects to a streaming platform (like YouTube, Twitch, etc.) via an internet connection.

Distribution: The server then distributes the stream to various content delivery networks (CDNs) to ensure efficient and reliable delivery to viewers across different locations. CDNs help manage traffic and reduce latency.

Playback: Viewers access the live stream through a platform (website, app, etc.) where the stream is embedded. Their devices decode the data and display the video and audio in real-time.

Monitoring/Management: Throughout the stream, technicians or operators monitor various metrics like viewership, stream health, and any potential technical issues. Adjustments might be made on the fly to maintain stream quality.

Interaction: Many live streams allow for real-time interaction, where viewers can comment, ask questions, or engage with the content creator. Moderators may manage these interactions.

Conclusion: Once the live stream concludes, the transmission is stopped, but the recorded stream might remain available for on-demand viewing.

Each of these steps requires careful planning, setup, and often troubleshooting to ensure a smooth live streaming experience for both content creators and viewers.

Advantages and limitations of Live Streaming

Advantages

- Real-Time Interaction: Viewers can engage with content creators or presenters in real time, fostering a sense of community and immediacy.
- Wider Reach: It enables a global audience to access content simultaneously, breaking geographical barriers.
- Versatility: Live streaming can cover various content types, from entertainment to education, sports, business events, and more.
- Cost-Effective: Compared to traditional broadcasting methods, live streaming can be more cost-effective, especially for smaller creators or businesses.
- Analytics and Feedback: Platforms often provide analytics, allowing creators to gauge audience engagement, gather feedback, and adjust content accordingly.
- Authenticity: Live streams offer an unfiltered, authentic experience, fostering trust and a closer connection between creators and viewers.

However, live streaming also has its limitations:

Limitations

- Technical Challenges: Reliability on a stable internet connection and technical equipment can be a hurdle. Issues like lag, buffering, or hardware failure can disrupt the streaming experience.
- Audience Accessibility: Not all viewers may have the required internet speed or access to watch live streams, limiting the potential audience.
- Monetization Complexity: While live streaming can be monetized, especially on platforms like Twitch or YouTube, it often requires meeting certain criteria or building a substantial audience.
- Content Control: Live content lacks the control of pre-recorded material. Mistakes or unforeseen incidents happen in real time and cannot be edited out.
- Time Sensitivity: Live streams are time-bound; missing the live event means missing out on the real-time interaction and experience.
- Legal and Regulatory Concerns: Depending on the content, live streaming may pose legal or regulatory challenges, especially regarding copyright infringement or sensitive material.

Understanding these advantages and limitations helps creators and businesses make informed decisions when utilizing live streaming as part of their content or communication strategy.

4

Kisan Call Centres and Community Radio

Pooja V

Department of Agricultural Extension Education
University of Agricultural Sciences, Raichur

Kisan Call Centre (1551)

The department of agriculture and cooperation (DAC) Ministry of agriculture, Government of India launched kisan call centres on January 21, 2004 across the country to deliver extension services to the farming community. It provides information in all major languages through toll-free telephone no 1551 and 1800180 1551 from 6 a.m. to 10.p.m. on all 7 days of a week. on BSNL routes. With a view to monitor the KCC activities a state level monitoring committee (SLMC) has been constituted in each KCC. Presently there are --- kccs in the country.

The kisan call centers consists of three levels

Level I: The first level operator is an agricultural graduate with a rural background and knows the local language. They are expected to answer a majority of questions asked by the farmers. The details of the question and answers are fed into computer by operator. In case the operator at level I is not able to satisfy the farmer, he forwards the call to the concerned subject matter specialist sitting anywhere in the state, in any institution, for giving advice.

Level II: It has subject matter specialists (SMS) who are at their respective place (Research stations, ATIC, KVK, agricultural colleges) of work. The I level operator forwards the call on 'call sharing mode' to level II centre & over 70% of questions form the I level get answered at this level. The data relating to the caller including the question asked is also be transferred to the Level-II functionary on his computer along with the call. In case, it is not possible to answer, there is a system to revert back to the caller by post / fax / e-mail or by telephone in 72 hours.

Level III: (The management group) It consists of a dedicated cell located at the nodal office. This receives the questions that have not been answered at the first and second levels as well as IVR calls (Interactive voice recording). Appropriate replies to these questions are framed in consultation with the concerned specialists available within or outside the state by the nodal cell. The replies are sent to farmers by post / e-mail / fax / phone within 72 hours of receipt of question.

Advantages

1. Since troll free number is provided, it does not involve any cost.
2. Farmers' problems can be solved quickly and even in emergent situation like epidemic of crop disease and pest; KCC is very useful medium for solution. 3. Clarification and additional query are possible because of direct contact established.
3. KCC can reduce the burden of extension personnel who are busy in official work due to inadequate extension staff
4. Complicated problems are taken to the scientists for further research and clarification.

Limitations

1. People find difficulty in establishing online connection
2. Less experienced staff at first level sends queries to second level causing delay in response.

Community Radio

Radio broadcasting with the objective of serving the cause of the community in the service area by involving members of the community in the broadcast of their programs. Community radio speeds up the process of informing the community and therefore acts as a catalyst of change. It serves as a watchdog on civic authorities/ power holders, providing a forum for active relationships between leaders and citizens. Community radio can change the behavior of its communities for the good.

Community radios were introduced with the following broad objectives

- Enhancing participation of the people in the development process.
- Capacity building in rural areas, through education.

- Providing opportunities for people to upgrade their skills and enhance their creative talents.
- Preserving and promoting traditional wisdom, knowledge and skills, thereby helping to promote and protect the local language, arts, crafts, culture and traditions.
- Bring within easy reach of the rural population, topical information in areas of agriculture, social welfare, education, health and environment.
- Help in creating rural networks for the rural cottage and village industry.
- The members of the community get an opportunity to express themselves socially, politically and culturally.
- Community radio encourages participatory community development, harnessing locally available resources and innovation in community development.

Community Radio in India

Sangam Community Radio

Sangam Community Radio launched on 15th October 2008 is the brainchild of the Deccan Development Society (DDS), a two-decade old grass root organization working in about 75 villages with women's groups in Medak district of Andhra Pradesh.

Initially, this Community Radio Station was set up with assistance from UNESCO in 1998-99. The station is located in the DDS 'Green School' campus in Pastapur village, Zaheerabad Mandal, Medak District, Andhra Pradesh. In the absence of a licensing policy, programmes produced by it were narrow casted through tape-recorders in the village sangams. It has a 100-watt transmitter which can reach a radius of 30 kms. The station is part of the Women Speak to Women programme of UNESCO, which has supported this venture. The operating staff of Sangham Radio consists of two coordinators with the help of 12 rural reporters. Deccan Development Society has built a low-cost radio station.

Different programmes broadcasted by Sangham Community Radio Station: Mana vuri pantalu, Mana bhasha, Ruchulu, Chiru dhanyalu, Folk songs, Yarandla muchatalu, Darvajala Davakhana, Vuri varthalu.

Krishi Community Radio

Krishi Community Radio (90.4 MHz) is the first Community Radio in India under State Agricultural Universities was established on 17th May 2007 under the University of Agricultural Sciences, Dharwad. It is recognized as one of the frequency modulations (FM) mediums for the transfer of agricultural technology to needy farmers in coverage areas.

Currently, there are around 188 operational community radio stations across the country, while a total of 400 have been approved by the government. Setting up one such radio station costs anywhere between Rs 15-20 lakh. As per the Community Radio Support Scheme, the government can grant 50% of the total estimated expenditure for setting up the radio station, up to a ceiling of Rs 7.50 lakh.

Namma Dawani Community Radio

Nama Diwani community radio in Kolar district of Karnataka was initiated by TOCEN Asus comment radio to address local information needs about government and school programmes. The Namma Dhawani project is mostly run by members of self-help groups. For training and capacity building the project was sported by All Bosdia Radio.

Kutch Mahila Vikas Sangathan in Bhuj

The UNDP and Kutch Mahila Vikas Sangathan (KMVS) in Gujarat have highlighted the communication programmes on the needs and aspirations of the community including traditional art and culture. The radio has been used as a medium to reinforce ethnic identity and promote community cohesion during times of religious tension.

Alternative for India Development (AID) in Daltonganj, Jharkhand

The AID project is supported by the National Foundation for India (NFL). The experiment has successfully used the radio as a medium to address governance issues, such as Ability or lack of responsiveness on the part of the administration.

Expert systems and Information kiosk

Expert Systems

Computer Programme designed to stimulate the problem-solving behavior of an expert in a narrow domain. (Or) "a system that uses human knowledge captured in a computer to solve problems that ordinarily require human expertise".

Main Component of ES: Crop doctor (image-based diagnosis).

Compontes of Expert Systems:

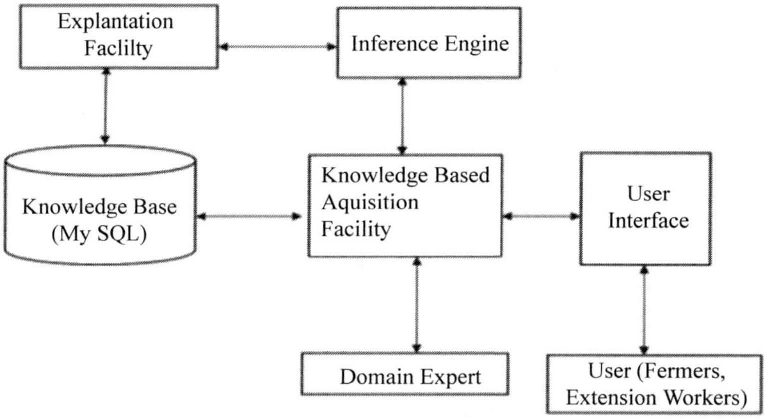

User interface: mechanism to support communication between the user and system

- **Explanation Facility:** explains the user about the reasoning process of the system. By keeping track of the rules that are fired, an explanation facility presents a chain of reasoning that led to a certain conclusion
- **Working memory**: This is a database used to store collection of facts which will be used later by the rules.
- **Inference Engine:** makes inferences. If the symptom of crop is X, Then the nutrition deficiency is Y.
- **Knowledge Acquisition Facility:** allows the user to enter knowledge in the system.

Capabilities of Expert Systems

- Explore the impact of strategic goals
- Impact of plans on resources
- Integrate general design principles and manufacturing limitations
- Provide advice on decisions
- Monitor quality and assist in finding solutions
- Look for causes and suggest solutions

Advantages of Expert System

- Expert system are useful in many aspects and ready to use by end users as advisory systems.
- Provides consistent answers for repetitive decisions, processes and tasks
- Holds and maintains significant levels of information.
- Encourages human expert to clarify and finalize the logic of their decision-making.

Limitations of Expert System

- Lacks common sense needed in some decision-making.
- Cannot make creative responses as human experts would in unusual circumstances.
- Domain experts are not always able to explain their logic and reasoning.
- Cannot adapt to changing environments, unless knowledge base is changed.

Agricultural Expert Systems in the World

1. **Soybean crop:** The expert system applied to the problems of diagnosing Soybean diseases in Illinois, USA is one of the earliest expert systems developed in agriculture
2. **POMME:** It is an expert system for apple orchid management. POMME advises growers about when and what to spray on apples to avoid infestations
4. **COMAX:** It is a crop management expert system for cotton. The expert Systems is integrated with a computer model, Gossym, that stimulates the growth of the cotton plat.
5. **CUPTEX:** An expert system developed for cucumber production management an used by the agricultural extension service within the Egyptian Ministry of Agriculture a private sector. CUPTEX is composed of three expert systems for fertigation plant care a disorder remediation.
6. **POMI:** In Italy, an expert system for integrated pest management of apple orchards
7. **CALEX:** It is an integrated expert decision support system for agricultural management developed at the University of California.

8. **LEY Expert System:** It is computer controlled, automated, remote, real-time weather data acquisition and reporting system in Washington State. Real-time weather data are also used in applications such as irrigation scheduling, crop protection and pest management.

Agriculture Expert System in India

1. **Wheat Crop:** Indian Agricultural Statistics Research Institute (IASRI) has developed an Expert System on Wheat Crop Management System (EXOWHEM) to diagnose pests and diseases for wheat crop and suggest preventive/curative measures.

2. **Rice Crop Doctor:** National Institute of Agricultural Extension Management (MANAGE) has developed an expert system to diagnose pest and diseases for rice crop and suggest preventive / curative measures. The rice crop doctor illustrates the use of expert- systems specifically in the area of rice production taking into consideration of a few major pest and diseases and some deficiency problems limiting the rice yield.

3. **Grape Cultivation:** Indian Institute of Horticultural Research, Bangalore developed an expert system for the grape cultivators.

4. **AGREX:** Centre for Informatics Research and Advancement, Kerala has prepared an expert system called AGREX to help agricultural field personnel give timely and correct advice to the farmers relating to fertilizer application, crop protection, irrigation scheduling, diagnosis of diseases in paddy and post harvest technology of fruits and vegetables.

Information Kiosks

A kiosk is a small, free-standing physical structure that displays information or provides a service. An information kiosk is a computer terminal featuring specialized hardware and software that provides access to information and applications for communication, commerce, entertainment, education and many more.

For e.g., at Acharya N. G. Ranga Agricultural University, the information kiosks were installed at the modern agricultural information centre and at Agricultural Technology Information Center (ATIC) with touch screen operation. Any visitor to the university can have access to any kind of information regarding the package of practices, plant protection, nutritional deficiencies, symptoms of various pests and diseases of a variety of crops and problems he encounters in the field.

Types of Kiosks

1. Financial services kiosk

The financial services kiosk can provide the ability for customers to perform transactions that may normally require a bank teller and may be more complex and longer to perform than desired at an ATM. These are sometimes to referred to as "bank-in-a-box. These units are generally referred to 'multi-function financial service kiosks.

2. Photo kiosk

An interactive kiosk which allows users to print pictures from their digital images. Two major classes of photo kiosks exist:

- **Digital Order Stations --** This type of photo kiosk exists within retail locations & allows users to place orders for prints and photographic products.
- **Instant Print Stations -** This type of photo kiosk uses internal printers to instantly create photographic prints for a self-serve paying customer. Often located in public locations (hotels, schools, airports), Instant Print Stations handle payments.

3. Internet kiosk

An Internet kiosk is a terminal that provides public Internet access. Internet kiosks sometimes resemble telephone booths, and are typically placed in settings such as hotel lobbies, long-term care facilities, medical waiting rooms, or airports for fast access to e mail or web pages.

4. Agriculture kiosk

Agri-kiosk is a one-stop shop for all agricultural needs providing services such as soil testing, seed selection, appropriate pesticides, herbicides, and fungicides. Agri-kiosks also provide the latest agricultural equipment on rent which make it easily accessible for women farmers.

5. Self-service kiosk

Self-service kiosks are interactive computer terminals that give customers access to information, such as inventory availability, menus, queuing, travel plans and more. There are different types of self-service kiosks, ranging from ruggedized tablets in secured enclosures to free-standing stations.

6. Ticketing kiosk

Many amusement parks such as Disney have unattended outdoor ticketing kiosks. Amtrak has automated self-service ticketing kiosks. Cruise ships use ticketing kiosks for passengers. The ticket halls of train stations and metro stations have ticketing kiosks that sell transit passes, train tickets, transit tickets, and train passes.

7. Visitor management and security kiosk

A visitor management and security kiosk can facilitate the visitor check-in process at businesses, schools, and other controlled access environments. These systems can check against blacklists, run criminal background checks, and print access badges for visitors.

8. Video kiosk

Video kiosk integrates video conferencing and collaboration capabilities to help users run video calls or conferences with available operators, view content or exchange messages. Video kiosks are often used in banking or telemedicine for improved customer service.

9. Information kiosk

Museums, historical sites, national parks and other tourist/visitor attractions often engage kiosks as a method for conveying information about a particular exhibit or site to the guests.

10. Tele-kiosk

The tele kiosk can be considered the technical successor to the telephone booth, a publicly accessible set of devices that are used for communication. These can include email, fax, SMS, as well as standard telephone service.

11. DVD vending kiosk

An example of a vending kiosk is that of the DVD rental kiosks manufactured by several manufacturers, where a user can rent a DVD, secured by credit card. One of the larger DVD Vending Kiosks companies is outer wall.

Advantages

- Convenient; easy to operate
- Large screen for navigation
- Kiosk's location-specific Ads
- Enhance customer satisfaction by providing needed web-based services.

- Acquires new customers via Sign-up/opening an account
- Educates new and existing customers about service & products
- Replaces the human assistants

Limitations

- Regular maintenance at intervals
- Initial hardware cost
- High installation & authorisation cost
- Customer difficulties are common
- Personal interaction is limited.

Community-owned Rural Internet Kiosks Importance

1. **Agricultural produce market rates:** Prevailing rates of prominent crops at the local and recognized markets around the country are available online for a nominal charge.
2. **Online registration of applications:** Villagers had to make several visits to the local revenue offices to file applications for obtaining certificates. This can be avoided with online facilities.
3. **Village auction site:** It provides auction facilities to farmers and villagers for land, agricultural machinery, equipment and other durable commodities. One can put one's commodity on sale for a nominal charge.
4. **Copies of land records:** Documents related to land records are provided on the spot at a nominal charge.
5. **Online public grievance redress:** A complaint can be filed and a reply received within 7 days for a nominal cost.

5

ICT Project Initiatives in Agriculture and Allied Sectors

Likhila B

Agricultural Economics, School of Agriculture
Mohan Babu University, Tirupathi

The intersection of Information and Communication Technologies (ICT) with agriculture has sparked a transformative revolution in the farming landscape. ICT projects in agriculture represent a paradigm shift, leveraging technological advancements to optimize farming practices, enhance productivity and ensure sustainable food production. From precision farming and data-driven decision-making to innovative tools and connectivity solutions, these projects harness the power of digital innovation to address challenges and drive efficiency across the agricultural sector. In this era where technology has become a cornerstone of progress, ICT projects stand as beacons of hope, ushering in a new era of smarter, more resilient and eco-conscious agriculture. The initiatives of ICT projects in agriculture and allied sectors

1. Warna wired village project

Started: 1998 by a non-governmental cooperative organization in Maharashtra.

Objective

- Provided internet access to cooperative societies spread in 70 villages of Maharashtra.
- The aim was to provide information to the villagers by establishing network booths in the villages.
- The Wrana project was an endeavour that was more broadly focused on the agricultural community's growth than it was on agriculture.
- Farmers could use six web-based applications from these booths, including automated help for filling out applications for government documents like ration cards and birth and death certificates, crop

information, water supply details, medical facilities, bus and train schedules and employment and agricultural schemes.

2. Villages Knowledge Centre (VKC)

Started: 2000, Pondicherry by MSSRF.

Objective

- M.S Swaminathan Research Foundation has established a hub of the information network, in Villianur village (Pondicherry) to cater to the information needs of the rural people.
- It is aimed at bringing the benefits of modern ICTs to rural families in Pondicherry.
- Gateway of technical information related to agriculture, input, prices of output, crop rotation, fertilizers, and pesticides.
- The "Hub and Spoke Model" give strength to the system
- Hub is a village resource center that is connected to 20-30 VKC spread over a 60 km radius.

3. Akashganga

Started: 1996, NDDB.

Objective

- A milk way between tradition and technology.
- Provides a total integrated solution for automatic milk collection.
- Help in timely milk collection and help in timely remuneration to farmers.

4. **The Dairy Information and Services Kiosk (DISK)**

Started: 1999, GCMFL (Gujarat Cooperative Milk Marketing Federation Ltd.) with IIM, Ahmadabad.

Objective

- The model includes a complete history of milk cattle owned by the member farmers.
- The details such as the breed and a history of diseases and artificial insemination are maintained in the system.

- It is being used at milk collection centres and in cooperatives to measure the fat content of milk, test the milk quality and make an instant payment to the farmers.

5. **Automated Milk Collection System (AMCS)**

Started: NDDB created software to connect many stakeholders at the DCS, Union, Federation, and national levels. The integrated structure offers both a mobile application for critical informatics and a collective provision for financial inclusion. There are already more than 25 milk unions in India using AMCS.

Objective

- To reduce the time required in collecting milk.
- Electronic techniques to weigh milk and measure the fat content.
- Maintain record at Dairy Cooperative Societies (DCS).

6. ITC e-Chaupaal

A private sector initiative Started in 2000 in Madhya Pradesh (MP). Around 4 million farmers are impacted by the 6,100 e-Chaupaal that are in use in 35,000 villages throughout 10 states (Madhya Pradesh, Haryana, Uttarakhand, Uttar Pradesh, Rajasthan, Karnataka, Kerala, Maharashtra, and Tamil Nadu).

- ITC Limited has launched the e-Chaupaal project to connect with rural farmers online for the purchase of agricultural and aquaculture products such soybeans, wheat, coffee and prawns.
- Now it is the largest initiative among internet-based interventions in the rural area.
- In rural communities throughout numerous agricultural regions of the nation, ITC Limited has set up computers and Internet connectivity. so that farmers can directly bargain with the company for the sale of their goods.
- Farmers who have access to the internet can order agricultural inputs like seeds and fertilizer as well as learn about appropriate farming methods and mandi prices.
- This aids farmers in raising the quality of their goods and lets them sell them for more money.
- It is for soybean farmers to provide real-time information.
- It eliminates wasteful intermediates.

7. **Bhoomi (Land Record Computerisation)**

Started: In 2000, the Karnataka state government put the project into action as part of the central government's Computerization of Land Records scheme.

Objective

- The state of Karnataka's land records is managed and accessible through Bhoomi, an online database and viewing system.
- It is a comprehensive database of significant documents and information, including ownership demarcation maps, the Record of Rights, Tenancy and Crop Inspection (RTC), also known as Pahani,
- and details regarding mutations, which is the change of title ownership from one party to another when a property is sold or transferred.

8. Gyandoot

Started: An intranet that was launched in January 2000 in the Dhar district of Madhya Pradesh, India.

Objective

- Gyandoot links rural cyber-kiosks that provide online government and agricultural services.
- The project aims to build technologically advanced, community owned, and long-lasting information kiosks in rural areas with a high level of poverty.
- To improve governance at the village, block, and district levels.
- Provide information to farmers like best practices related to agriculture and the price of products in a different market.
- The project involved setting up of low cost potentially selfsustainable community owned rural intranet terminal known as "soochanalya".

9. e-Sagu

Started: 2004, an ICT-based personalized agro-advisory system.

Objective

- The word 'Sagu' means 'cultivation' in the Telugu language.
- It aims to expand farm productivity by timely distributing highquality personalized agro-expert advice to each farm at the farmer's door-step.
- The advices are provided typically once a week

- Aims to solving the problem from sowing to harvesting which reduces the cost of cultivation and increases the farm productivity as well as quality of agri-commodities.

10. ISRO -Village Resource Centres (VRCs)

Indian Satellite Research Organization (ISRO) has initiated Village Resource Centres (VRCs) with a view to integrating its capabilities in satellite communications and satellite-based earth observations to disseminate a variety of services to address the changing and critical needs of rural communities in 2006.

Village Resource Centres (VRCs) was inaugurated in 2004. Under this VRC programme, most of the MSSRF -VKCs are connected through Indian Space Research Organization's (ISRO) uplink and downlink satellite facilities. Village Resource Centres are single window delivery mechanisms for tele-medicine, tele-education, natural resources data, agriculture advisories, land & water resources advisories, interactive farmers' advisories, e-governance services and weather advisories. It also involves capacity building of the community to enhance its awareness and knowledge levels. The VRCs provide information on health, education, nutrition, gender issues, legal services and women empowerment.

11. AQUA (Almost All Questions Answered)

It is a Farmer Knowledge Exchange Forum in the website (http://aaqua.org) where any farmer, agriculturist or hobbyist can register and post questions and a panel of agricultural experts answer these questions Information such as geographical location, weather, and season are reviewed automatically and made available to experts. Questions can be asked in one of four languages: Hindi, English, Kannada, and Marathi. It is a problem-solving system dedicated to find solutions to problems posed by Indian farmers. Answers to agricultural related queries are sent in 24 to 72 hours depending on the difficulty.

12. AGRISNET (Agricultural Informatics and Communication Network)

It is a mission mode project under national e-governance plan of the Govt. of India. It provides relevant information and services to the farming communities and private sectors through the use of ICT, to supplement the existing channels. The end users can access information through an online platform at their doorsteps. The website address is http://www.wbagrisnet.gov.in/

13. AGMARKNET (Agricultural Marketing Information System Network)

It is an ICT project of the Directorate of Marketing and Inspection (DMI), Govt. of India started in the 9th Plan. This project has networked 735 Agricultural Produces Wholesale Markets, 75 State Agricultural Marketing Board / Directorate and DMI Regional Offices during 2000-02 and embarked upon additional 2000 markets during 10th Plan period (2002- 2007). The website is http://agmarkenet.nic.in/.

14. E-Krishi

It is a market driven agricultural initiative through IT enabled agribusiness u Kerala. It was implemented by Kerala State IT Mission and Indian Institute of Info Technology and Management, Kerala in collaboration with the Department of A (http://e-krishi.org/sit

15. DISK (Dairy Information and Services Kiosk)

It is a web based personalized agro-advisory system which uses IT to wives unscientific agricultural practices (Sagu means cultivation in Telugu and E-Sag electronic cultivation). It is a cost effective agricultural information dissemination sys and a joint research project of Media Lan Asia and IIIT, Hyderabad. It is one of the successful initiatives taken by the Gujarat Co-operative Milk Marke Federation Ltd. with the help of IIM, Ahmedabad. The DISK module includes a comp history of dairy cattle owned by the member farmers. Detailed information on breed, history of disease incidence, vaccination and artificial insemination are maintained in the system s being used in the milk collecting centres and in cooperatives to measure the quality of mik including butter fat and promptly make the payment to the farmers. The websites http://www.iimahd.ernet.in/egov

16. Kissan Kerala

It is an innovative project launched by the Department of Agriculture, Govt. of Kerala. aimed to enhance total agriculture development and farmers' welfare in the State Website: http://kissankerala.net.

17. Self-Employed Women's Association (SEWA)

The Self-Employed Women's Association is a trade union representing poor, self employed women workers. SEWA was established in 1972. It has a membership of around 2,12,000 women spread over 790 villages in nine districts of Gujarat. Most of the areas where SEWA works are: drought-prone desert areas, where there is lack of employment, low wages poor health, low literacy.

SEWA supports its members to organize into groups or cooperatives, development and strengthening of Women Self-Help Groups (SHGs) and empowerment of women. Women empowerment is done using satellite communication for training and credit mobilization. SEWA plans to institutionalize the SATCOM training programme to build its cadre of barefoot managers on the following subjects:

1. Organizing training for capacity building
2. Women and panchayat raj
3. Women and forestry
4. Women and water
5. Savings and women.

SEWA is an institution of totally downtrodden women, which is now trying to expand its reach through modern ICT.

18. DACNET Project of the Department of Agriculture and Information Technology

The Department of Agriculture and Cooperation (DAC), Ministry of Agriculture has launched a project called DACNET for strengthening of information technology infrastructures with the help of National Informatics Centre (NIC), Department of Information Technology, Ministry of Communication and IT. The DACNET has four major components:

1. Networking of Directorates, Regional Directorates and Field Units for internet and intranet access with the Central Project Unit.
2. Establishment of LAN in Directorates / Regional Directorates, and PC client system.
3. IT empowerment of employees through specialized training programmes
4. Development of web-based applications software for strengthening e-governance applications.

19. Nandini (ICT for livestock productivity)

Started: In 2 blocks of Orrisa Jagatsinghpur and Balikuda.

Objective

- To improve the productivity of livestock by establishing a system of animal identification, registration and performance.

- For effective service delivery to farmers.
- A web-based portal facilities a Decision Support System (DSS) to government department for planning of different interventions.

20. Honey bee knowledge network

Under the honey bee knowledge network of Indian Institute of Management, Ahmedabad a large number of grass root inventions (Indigenous technical knowledge or ITKs) have been identified and documented as short multimedia presentations. Database is created for these innovations and these are made accessible via wide area network.

6

Mobile Applications in Agricultural Extension

Karravula Rakesh

College of Agriculture, Rajendranagar
Professor Jayashankar Telangana State Agricultural University, Hyderabad

M-Agriculture

Mobile phones have changed the scenario of telecommunication. It is a source of communication for fast dissemination of information. Today, mobile usage has enabled farming communities to access agricultural and other business information without travelling long distances or reducing costs, time and money. Keeping in view the lower ratio of the farmer to the extension worker (1000: 1) and the inability of the extension workers to guide the farmers as per their information needs, the new concept of m-Agriculture (m-Krishi) has emerged at the beginning of twenty-first century all over the world including India.

Concept of m-Agriculture

m-Agriculture is IT enabled service based on a linear model of communication of agricultural technology which involves four main components: sender, message, channel and receiver. It usually sends instant bulk messages of agricultural technology to the farmers, agro-input providers and extension personnel through bulk Short Message Service (SMS). Bulk SMS is a special type of system by which an institution or organisation becomes able to send or receive a large volume of SMS i.e. SMS in bulk.

Advantages of SMS of Mobile Phone

1. As a channel it can provide up-to-date information on agriculture and allied sector is not possible by extension personnel.
2. As a tool for quick and timely information despatch which extension personnel.

3. For timely and wider interaction between and among researchers, extension and farmers.
4. It can help in reducing information cost, time and money of the farmers.
5. It can provide need-based information any time day in, day out.
6. It has a message storage facility.
7. Messages can be delivered in local languages.

The farmers can get a variety of services through SMS. Important services available through SMS relating to agriculture are:

- Availability of inputs
- Plant protection measures
- Livestock production and management
- Market information
- Weather forecast
- Disease forecast
- Information on training programme etc.

Development of mobile applications

A mobile application, most referred to as an "App", is a type of application software designed to run on a mobile device, such as a smartphone or tablet computer. Mobile application development is the set of processes and procedures involved in writing software for small, wireless computing devices, such as smartphones and other hand-held devices.

Mobile application development is the process of making software for smartphones, tablets and digital assistants, most commonly for the Android and iOS operating systems. The software can be preinstalled on the device, downloaded from a mobile app store or accessed through a mobile web browser. A mobile app development framework is a software framework that provides a platform to develop mobile applications. It provides the foundation and the structure to build scalable mobile apps.

The mobile app development process is as follows

- Choose a mobile app concept that offers a strong value and addresses user needs, increasing competitiveness in the market through uniqueness.

- Finalize the tech stack for app development, determining the methodology (Progressive Web, Native, Hybrid, or Cross-Platform) and selecting the framework (e.g., React Native) based on successful examples like Instagram and Facebook.
- Select appropriate app development tools based on project requirements.
- Commence app development using Agile methodology for efficient progress.
- Develop a prototype for stakeholder or investor feedback, conducting various tests (interruption, functional, performance, installation, memory) to refine the app based on feedback.
- Release the app for official beta testing after comprehensive checks, incorporating user corrections and multiple reviews before deployment. Establish mechanisms for ongoing customer feedback and support.
- Launch the app, focusing on optimization for the app store. Implement a detailed marketing strategy and App Store Optimization (ASO) to enhance visibility and increase downloads.
- Ensure regular maintenance and updates to address bugs, introduce patches, and integrate new features in line with current mobile app trends to sustain app relevance and performance.

Application of m-Agriculture

1. Kisan Mobile Sandesh (KMS)

The Krishi Vigyan Kendra Chhindwara, Madhya Pradesh and KVK Mahasamund Chhattisgarh have pioneered for the first time. They provided IT enabled services, Kisan Mobile Sandesh which was started on 26th August 2007 and in 2009 respectively. The Kisan Mobile Sandesh disseminating instant bulk messages from KVK to individual farmers, extension personnel and agro-input providers for extending agricultural information through bulk SMS. Messages are being delivered in Hindi and English. The messages are issued on agricultural development like weather forecast, disease forecast, availability of input, plant protection measures, market information, livestock production management, training programmes etc.

2. Kisan Mobile Advisory (KMA)

Kisan Mobile Advisory is a new initiative in using Information Communication Technology for dissemination of need-based and timely information to the farmers. In India mobile advisory services through 300 KVKS were launched.

Regular mobile advisory services with regard to information on weather, market and farm operations are provided to farmers in 300 districts located in eight Zones of the country. The Kisan Mobile Advisory has made access to the information easier and cost effective to the farmers. Important messages on plant protection, production techniques, horticulture, animal husbandry, weather forecast etc. are disseminated timely and quickly to the farmers

m-Krishi (Mobile phone-based ICT)

Mobile Agro Advisory System (m-Krishi) can provide information on weather, soil, pesticides that are specific to farmers' plot. Farmers can receive information on micro climate, local market price, crops available in the market, availability of seeds and other relevant information on a mobile phone. The m-Krishi application enables farmers to send queries, comprising of text, voice, and pictures specific to their land and crop to agricultural experts using their mobile phone. Farmers can also send pictures of their crops and pests captured with mobile phone cameras; sensors provide farm specific soil and crop data, and weather stations provide micro climatic details. After analysis of available information, the expert's advice on the farmers' query is provided on the farmer's mobile phone.

Mobile-based agriculture apps

1. Kisan Suvidha

It was first released in March of 2016. The app is accessible in a number of different languages. It was created by the Ministry of Agriculture and Farmers Welfare and the Department of Agriculture and Cooperation in order to assist farmers by providing them with timely information.

Market prices, seeds, pesticides, fertilisers, weather, input dealers, and agricultural machinery are among the topics covered. Market prices are provided, as well as information on the rates of various commodities in various mandis. It delivers a current day weather report as well as a five-day weather forecast for a selected district. This app also includes information on severe weather.

2. e-NAM

With the purpose of "One Nation-OneMarket," it was launched on April 14, 2016. It's an agricultural produce computerised trading programme that aims to build a united national market. Through an online bidding mechanism, it assists farmers in determining a transparent price for their produce. By March 2018, all 585 APMCs (Agriculture Produce Market Committees) have joined to e-NAM. There are 1000 Mandis registered under e-NAM (One Nation-One Market) in 18 states and two UTs (1000 more mandis to be integrated by 2021-22). Small Farmer Agribusiness Consortium is the major proponent of e-NAM (SFAC). Rajasthan has the most e-NAM Mandi's. In April 2020, new e- NAM modules were released.

- Warehouse based trading module: e- NAM integrated with e-Negotiable Warehouse receipts.
- FPO Module: Uploading of produce, bidding, and payment from their collection centers directly.

3. Meghdoot

It was released on the 7th of August, 2019. The India Meteorological Department (IMD), the Indian Institute of Tropical Meteorology (IITM), and the Indian Council of Agricultural Research (ICAR) have collaborated on these projects. Meghdoot gives current, historical, and anticipated weather data for the next five days, including temperature, rainfall, humidity, wind speed, and direction, all of which are important in agricultural activities. So that farmers may adjust their field operations to changing weather conditions and reduce crop losses.

It also supplies farmers with crop advisories based on meteorological data. Both local and English language advisories are accessible. Every Tuesday and Friday, Agro Met Field Units (AMFU) release district-level crop and animal management warnings based on expected weather information. Meghdoot will assist farmers in making weather-sensitive decisions such as crop planting, fertiliser application, pesticide application, irrigation scheduling, sale of produce, and animal immunisation, among other things.

4. Mausam

It was released in the year 2021. The India Meteorological Department (IMD), the International Crops Research Institute for the Semi-Arid Tropics (ICRISAT), and the Indian Institute of Tropical Meteorology collaborated to design and develop it (IITM).

It will provide current weather information in 200 cities, such as rainfall, temperature, humidity, wind speed, and direction. Eight times a day, the information will be delivered. It will also provide three-hourly nowcasts for local meteorological phenomena and their severity for around 800 stations and areas. The impact of severe weather will be included in the warning if it occurs.

Weather data from the previous 24 hours will also be available on the app. It also has a system in place that would send out color-coded alerts (red, yellow, orange) for all districts twice a day for up to five days in advance of bad weather.

5. Gemini

A new satellite-based GEMINI system has been launched by the Airport Authority of India (AAI) and the Indian National Centre for Ocean Information Services (INCOIS) to inform deep-sea fishermen of disasters. It is a 'hail-proof' portable device linked to ISRO satellites.

Deep-sea fishermen rely on the satellite-based GEMINI system for critical messages and alerts. All important messages and warnings will be transmitted via GAGAN, which will be received and transferred to a mobile phone by the selected device. The information would subsequently be decoded and displayed to the fisherman by the appropriate mobile application. It can be translated into nine other languages. Fishermen who are outside of their phone company's signal range might use this technique to get warnings and alerts. The range of mobile phone frequencies is limited to 10-12 km, but with GEMINI, this can be extended to 300 nautical miles.

6. Kisan Rath

The Ministry of Agriculture and Farmers Welfare launched this app in April of 2020. During the covid-19 pandemic, the app assists farmers and traders in determining the best means of transportation for the transit of agricultural produce. By the end of April 2020, the app will have registered 80,474 farmers and 70,581 dealers (4).

7. Agmarknet

It was established in the year 2000 with the goal of creating a nationwide information network for the rapid broadcast and collecting of market data and information for efficient and timely use. It uses ICT as a tool of extension to assist farmers in responding to new problems posed by commodity price changes. Improve agricultural marketing efficiency through regular training and extension to reach farmers in specific regions in their native tongue.

8. Digital Mandi

Appkiddo is the creator of this app. This app displays the most recent Mandi agricultural commodity prices published from several districts and states in India. It categorises commodities by product or state by state. The farmer can browse through several commodity categories and obtain price information for the selected commodity as provided by various states/mandis.

- Farmers can obtain information on commodity prices in various states/ mandis.
- It had a straightforward process for determining the mandi price of the selected commodity.
- It will duplicate a commodity's mandi price and broadcast it on social media.
- It will sync data from the Indian government's Agmarknet.nic. in-app.

9. Plantix

PEAT created this app for local crop needs in partnership with ICRISAT and State Agricultural University, and it was released in Telugu. It focuses on disease detection and tracking. It provides people all over the world with personalised information on best practises, preventative measures, and independent action alternatives. It allows users to send photographs of afflicted plants directly from their smartphones and walks them through a simple diagnosis process to determine the plant disease. All photos supplied through the Mobile App are geotagged, allowing for real-time pest and disease monitoring.

Real-time diagnosis: Crop shots are evaluated using image-recognition technology that searches a library of half a million images covering 30 crops and provides prescriptions for more than 120 crop illnesses. It also had features such as a weather information system, a community component that allows for easier engagement, and smallholder farmers as end-users: It's completely free, and it comes with an easy-to-use dashboard in local languages.

10. Iffco Kisan Agriculture

This software provides access to a variety of modules such as agricultural advise, weather, market pricing, and an agriculture information library in the form of text, photographs, audio, and videos in the language of choice. It provides phone numbers for contacting Kisan Call Centre Services. The software is available in eleven Indian languages, including English. It also includes weather, market price, and agro advisory information. It contained Ask the Experts, Agri Library, and Market Access features.

11. Pusa Krishi

ICAR-IARI developed it. It encourages agribusiness ventures by promoting technological research and commercialization for all types of businesses, from corporations to individual farmers. Farmers are given knowledge on novel crop types created by the Indian Council of Agricultural Research (ICAR), resource-saving cultivation practises, farm machinery and their deployment, and production technology. Farmers can communicate with stakeholders in real time thanks to a feedback section.

12. Bhuvan Hailstorm

The Ministry of Agriculture and Farmers Welfare, Government of India, developed it. This mobile app was created to record crop loss as a result of hailstorms, as well as images and geographic coordinates. An Agriculture Officer would go out into the field with a smartphone or tablet loaded with this software and collect field data for hailstorm damage assessment. This mobile app may take a picture of a field with the latitude and longitude, as well as the name of the crop, the date of sowing, the date of expected harvesting, and the source of irrigation. The recorded data is instantly plotted in Bhuvan Portal, allowing for easy analysis.

13. Crop Insurance

Department of Agriculture and Farmers Welfare launched it on December 23, 2015. Crop insurance information is provided in this app. It can be used to calculate Insurance Premiums for notified crops based on area, coverage amount, and loan amount if the farmer is a loanee. It can also be used to obtain information on any notified crop's normal sum insured, extended sum insured, premium details, and subsidy information in any notified area. This app is bilingual (Hindi and English). (4).

14. Atmanirbhar Krishi

The Tech Mahindra Makers Lab team created this. The Atmanirbhar Krishi App was introduced on June 29, 2021, to give farmers with relevant agricultural information and early weather notifications. The Atmanirbhar Krishi App now has access to information vital to farmers curated by several government ministries on the national digital platform 'KisanMitr.' **Features:**

- Available in 12 languages
- Free for farmers, start-ups, KVKs, SHGs, and NGOs
- Uses minimal bandwidth to address connectivity issues
- Does not collect any inputs from the farmer
- Relies on the farmers' geo-location
- Data relevant to other locations can be gathered by entering the Pincode of that specific area both Android and Windows platforms are supported (11).

15. Agri App

Agri App is a ground-breaking Android-based mobile app. It contains comprehensive information on crop production, crop protection, and other agriculture-related services. Agri App is both an information site and an online market place, bringing together farmers, agricultural inputs, retail, and fulfilment services on a single digital platform. The Kannada, English, Hindi, Telugu, Tamil, and Marathi versions of the Agri App are now available. Features of this apps 1. Package of Practices 2. Chat 3. Videos 4. News 5. Discounts 6. Secure Payments 7. Promotions 8. Settings (12).

16. Pashu Poshan

Developed by the National Dairy Development Board (NDDB). This app helps to formulate a balanced ration while optimizing the cost considering the animal profile. A dairy farmer can use this software to determine the proper quantity and mix of feed and fodder to feed his dairy animals (13).

17. ICAR Technologies

Launched by ICAR. Consists of proven technologies generated by ICAR institutions. An easy way to locate appropriate technologies based on major resource, commodity and technology groups (5).

18. m Hariyali

Launched by the Ministry of Jal Shakti with the aim of cleaning and greening open space through plantation, rainwater harvesting awareness and construction.

19. mKisan

It was launched by the Ministry of Agriculture and Farmers Welfare to allow all Central and State government entities in the agriculture and related sectors to provide farmers information, services, and advisories by SMS in their preferred language, agricultural practises, and location.

20. Krishi

New ICT initiative of ICAR. The Indian Council of Agricultural Research (ICAR) launched the Agricultural Knowledge Resources and Information System Hub for Innovations to centralize access to its knowledge resources for all stakeholders. The app is being created as an ICAR-wide, consolidated data repository system for technology, data from experiments, surveys, observational research, geospatial data, publications, and educational resources.

Website, BLOG and Portals

Website

Websites serve as the digital storefronts of the modern era, acting as a gateway for individuals and businesses to establish an online presence. A website is a collection of web pages and related content that is identified by a common domain name and published on at least one web server. Websites are designed to be accessed through a network, typically the internet, using a web browser.

There are various types of websites, each serving different purposes and catering to specific audiences. Here are some common types of websites:

- **E-commerce Websites:** These platforms facilitate online transactions, allowing businesses to sell products or services directly to consumers. Examples include Amazon, eBay, and Shopify.
- **Informational Websites:** Informational sites provide content on specific topics, offering valuable information to users. These could include educational websites, news portals, or informational blogs.
- **Portfolio Websites:** These showcase an individual's or a company's work, such as artists, designers, photographers, or agencies. They display samples of past projects or work achievements.
- **Blog or Personal Websites:** Blogs are platforms where individuals or groups regularly post content on various topics. They often include personal experiences, opinions, or niche interests.
- **Social Media Websites:** These platforms enable users to create profiles, connect with others, and share content. Examples include Facebook, Twitter, LinkedIn, and Instagram.
- **Business or Corporate Websites:** These websites represent a company or business and serve as a digital presence to provide information about their services, products, and contact details.
- **Educational Websites:** Educational platforms offer courses, learning materials, or resources for students, teachers, or lifelong learners. Examples include Coursera, Khan Academy, and Duolingo.
- **Media Sharing Websites:** Platforms that allow users to upload and share various media types like videos (YouTube), images (Instagram), or presentations (SlideShare).
- **Government Websites:** Managed by government agencies, these websites provide information about services, laws, regulations, and official documents.

- **Forums or Community Websites:** Websites that allow users to interact, discuss, and share information on specific topics or interests, often in a threaded discussion format.

Each type of website serves a unique purpose, catering to the diverse needs of users in the digital landscape, contributing significantly to the way information is accessed, shared, and utilized on the internet.

Web portals

A web portal is a web-based platform that collects information from several different sources and streamlines them into a single access point for information. It also often serves as the single point of access for information, a library of personalized and categorized content. It provides information catered from various sources such as emails, online forums, and search engines on one platform, uniformly.

The process of creating a web portal

1. **Planning stage:** There's a need to define whom, why and when the web portal is being built for. Specifications on how the information is easy-to-access, personalized to stakeholders' needs, secured, and up-to-date has to be taken care of.

2. **Know the Features to be Incorporated:** Customize the portal with more and more features. In a business portal one can incorporate Chatbots for Customer service, photo gallery, newsletters, advertisements, best buys, customer profiles, and more. Finalize features and functionalities for your web portal.

3. **Hire the Right Resource: Hiring the right resources**, explaining to them the exact needs and taking in their technical input in your project is easier as it is not within our capabilities. A leading web development company has a broad understanding of the industry and specialized skills.

4. **Add integrations:** This stage involves connecting all the tools you or your users need to accomplish their goals into the portal. Depending on your use case, this could include custom software or even SaaS products.

5. **Testing and Launching Your Web Portal:** Before deployment, experienced developers thoroughly test portal applications for errors, missing requirements, and instability issues. Once the bugs and errors are resolved, your business web portal is deployed on the internet.

6. **Timely maintenance is Inevitable:** Maintenance and support are a must to keep your web portal trending and most sought after among your target audience. This step will help you achieve milestones in the long run.

Writing for web portals

A distinctive writing style is needed for websites. Novelists use words to describe a scene. The news is covered by journalists with theatrical flair. Academics use citations to contextualize complicated concepts. Writers of web content communicate information as briefly as feasible.

1. **Write clearly:** It is recommended to avoid using long, complex sentences that attempt to explain something in complex words that may be explained in a simpler way. Simple sentences are best.
2. **Employ keywords:** Make use of words that are frequently utilised to describe your subject. Try to limit your use of proprietary terminologies and acronyms.
3. **Employ pronouns:** A user is "you." We refer to the business or government body. As a result, the content is easier to understand and has clearer sentence structure.
4. **Employ visuals, flowcharts, or multimedia:** It is simpler to absorb content when thoughts are represented visually. The text on your page should be supported by videos and photos.
5. **Employ headings**: Use headers and subheadings to break up your text and make it easier for visitors to access information.
6. **Segregate various concepts into distinct paragraphs:** Readers find lengthy, dense chunks of text frightening. A few concise paragraphs are superior to one lengthy one.
7. **Make links obvious to see:** Links ought to have a unified colour scheme and design. A link's colour shouldn't be altered to make it stand out. Nothing should be highlighted since it can be mistaken for a link.
8. **Talk in an active tone**: Not "The regulation was proposed by the board," but "The board proposed the legislation."
9. **Make use of numbered lists and bullets:** Use this for more than just extensive lists; one sentence with two bullets is simpler to read than three.

Blogs

Blogs are regularly updated websites that provide insight into a certain topic. The word blog is a combined version of the words "web" and "log." At their inception, blogs were simply an online diary where people could keep a log about their daily lives on the web. They have since morphed into an essential forum for individuals and businesses alike to share information and updates.

A blog (a shortened version of "weblog") is an online journal or informational website displaying information in reverse chronological order, with the latest posts appearing first, at the top. It is a platform where a writer or a group of writers share their views on an individual subject.

Blogging is a collection of skills that one needs to run and supervise a blog. This entails equipping a web page with tools to make the process of writing, posting, linking, and sharing content easier on the internet.

Types of Blogs

Blogs come in various forms, each tailored to different content, audiences, and purposes. Here are some common types of blogs:

- Personal Blogs: These blogs are a reflection of an individual's experiences, thoughts, opinions, and interests. They can cover a wide range of topics, from lifestyle and travel to personal development and hobbies.
- Lifestyle Blogs: Lifestyle blogs focus on various aspects of everyday life, including fashion, beauty, health, fitness, home decor, and family.
- Travel Blogs: Travel bloggers share their experiences, tips, and advice related to travel destinations, itineraries, accommodations, and cultural insights.
- Food Blogs: Food bloggers create content centered around recipes, cooking tips, restaurant reviews, dietary information, and culinary experiences.
- Parenting Blogs: Parenting bloggers share their experiences, tips, and advice related to raising children, family life, education, and parenting challenges.
- Technology Blogs: Tech bloggers cover topics related to gadgets, software reviews, tech news, troubleshooting guides, and industry insights.

- Finance and Business Blogs: These blogs focus on financial advice, investment strategies, business tips, entrepreneurship, and industry trends.
- Health and Wellness Blogs: Health bloggers discuss topics such as fitness routines, mental health, nutrition, wellness trends, medical advice, and self-care practices.
- DIY and Crafts Blogs: DIY bloggers offer tutorials, tips, and ideas for various crafts, hobbies, home improvement projects, and creative endeavors.
- Educational Blogs: Educational bloggers create content related to teaching, learning resources, educational tools, academic advice, and educational technology.
- Niche-Specific Blogs: These blogs cater to highly specialized interests such as pet care, gardening, sustainable living, photography, book reviews, and more.

The diversity of blog types allows individuals to find and create content that resonates with their interests, passions, and expertise, fostering communities and sharing valuable information in various domains.

Guidelines for writing blogs

Understand Your Audience: Gain insights into your audience's preferences and tailor content to their needs.

Craft Compelling Headlines: Create attention-grabbing headlines that entice readers to delve into your content.

Organize with Clarity: Structure your content using headers, subheaders, and bullet points for easy navigation.

Begin with an Engaging Introduction: Capture attention from the outset with an intriguing hook or relatable story.

Provide Value: Offer well-researched, informative content that delivers solutions, insights, or answers to your audience's queries.

Enhance with Visuals: Incorporate relevant images, videos, or infographics to add visual interest and aid comprehension.

Write Concisely and Clearly: Keep sentences and paragraphs concise, using straightforward language to maintain clarity.

Support with Examples: Bolster your points with real-life examples or case studies to provide credibility and context.

Include a Clear Call-to-Action: Guide readers on the next steps, whether it's subscribing, commenting, or exploring related content.

Optimize for SEO: Integrate relevant keywords naturally throughout your content to improve search engine visibility.

Proofread and Edit: Thoroughly review your content for errors in grammar, spelling, and factual accuracy. Edit for coherence and flow.

Maintain Consistency: Sustain a consistent tone, style, and publishing schedule to cultivate a loyal readership.

Promote Your Blog: Share your content across social media platforms, forums, or relevant communities to broaden its reach and engagement.

7

Social Media in Agriculture

Maibam Suraj Singh

Agricultural Extension, School of Social Sciences
College of Post Graduate Studies in Agricultural Sciences, Umaim
CAU, Imphal, Manipur

Social media are electronic communication platforms that allow users to interact, create, share, retrieve and exchange information and ideas in different forms.

Social media refers to the means of interactions among people in which they create, share, and/or exchange information and ideas in virtual communities and networks.

There are many forms of social media including blogs, micro-blogs, wikis, social networking sites, photo-sharing sites, instant messaging, video-sharing sites, podcasts, widgets, virtual worlds, and more. Ex: Facebook, Twitter, Instagram, LinkedIn and Youtube etc.,

Role of social media in Transfer of Technology

1. For personal and professional communication (whatsup)
2. To get latest information about agriculture events and news (ICAR – Twitter)
3. To exchange knowledge in agriculture and allied sectors (ICAR Websites, Pusa krishi, whatsup groups)
4. Act as a discussion platform for identifying solution and decision making etc.,
5. To promote new technologies in agriculture and allied sectors. (Agri innovative India, Pusa krishi incubator).
6. Highly cost-effective, simultaneously reaches large numbers of clients.
7. Location and client-specific, problem-oriented focusing on the user-generated content and discussion among the community members.

8. Easily accessed from mobile phones and hence, increases the internet presence of extension organizations and their client reach by making it accessible to all.
9. Brings all stakeholders into a single platform.
10. Can measure reach and success by tracking the number of visitors, friends, followers, mentions, likes, conversation index and number of shares.

Types of Social media

1. Social Networks

Social networking sites help people connect with each other and offer a multitude of ways for different brands to attract individuals. Users can share their thoughts, form groups based on their interests, curate content, upload photos and videos and participate in group discussions. It can reach wide and diverse audiences with advertisements and persuade influential people with the right targeting metrics. Examples of social networking platforms

Facebook: is a social media network that connects people through an online platform. By sharing content like text status posts, images, videos and external links like blog posts, Facebook users can contribute ideas and join conversations with other people who share the same or different interests

Instagram: Instagram is a free, online photo-sharing application and social network platform that was acquired by Facebook in 2012. Instagram allows users to edit and upload photos and short videos through a mobile app.

Twitter: Twitter is a service for friends, family, and coworkers to communicate and stay connected through the exchange of quick, frequent messages. People post Tweets, which may contain photos, videos, links, and text. These messages are posted to your profile, sent to your followers, and are searchable on Twitter search.

LinkedIn: LinkedIn is the world's largest professional network on the internet. It can be used LinkedIn to find the right job or internship, connect and strengthen professional relationships, and learn the skills which is need to succeed in a user career.

2. Discussion Forums

Discussion forums encourage people to answer each other's questions and share ideas and news. Many of these social media sites focus on posing questions to solicit the best answer. Answering them correctly and honestly can increase your credibility on the forum. That credibility and respect could lead to an increase in visits to your business or product website. You can also use discussion forums to do market research by asking people what they think of your products and brand. This can help you create more focused marketing campaigns. Examples of discussion forums:

Reddit: is an American social news aggregation, content rating, and discussion website. Registered users (commonly referred to as "Redditors") submit content to the site such as links, text posts, images, and videos, which are then voted up or down by other members. Posts are organized by subject into user-created boards called "communities" or "subreddits". Submissions with more upvotes appear towards the top of their subreddit and, if they receive enough upvotes, ultimately on the site's front page. Reddit administrators moderate the communities. Moderation is also conducted by community-specific moderators, who are not Reddit employees.

Digg: is a social network and news aggregating site. Users submit stories for promotion, and they are subsequently either voted for (digged) or against (buried). The most popular stories are posted to the front page, which can drive a lot of traffic to the corresponding sites. Ostensibly, the company's goal is to help users navigate an increasingly saturated media environment, making it easier to identify and consume the most important stories, videos, and Internet trends of the day.

Quora: Quora allows users to ask and answer questions, and each question is assigned to a specific a category. Users can proclaim themselves as experts in certain categories. The questions and answers posted on Quora can be rated negatively or positively by users. As a result, well-rated, helpful, Q-and-A threads are highlighted and appear more frequently in user's feeds. The comment function allows users to participate or discuss the topic of the post. In addition, Quora also provides **a** change feature that allows users to edit and improve foreign language questions and answers.

3. Image-sharing Networks

These social media sites let people share photos and related content. They offer a platform to start conversations, inspire creativity, make products seem more appealing and encourage customers to talk about your brand. For example, a clothing company could give everyone who posts a picture of their gear on the image-sharing network a chance to win a gift certificate. Examples of image-sharing networks:

Flickr: It is an online photo management and sharing application. It allows you to upload photos and share, edit, organize, and geotag them, as well as create your own galleries and develop image-based projects.

Photobucket: It is a web-based image and video hosting platform designed to help businesses share and store images securely. It lets users store non-compressed original photographs in the cloud for future reference. Key features include asset sharing, file conversion, asset library, search or filter and mobile application.

4. Bookmarking Networks

Bookmarking networks are platforms where users save different ideas, articles, posts and other content for later use. Many people also share links to lists of online resources. The purpose of these websites is to discover new content based on shared interests and to discuss trends. These networks can be used to direct people to website, engage them and influence their opinion by sharing content to bookmark. Examples of bookmarking networks:

Feedly: Feedly can aggregate or collect RSS feeds. An RSS feed enables the websites to publish information once and syndicate it automatically amongst the subscribers. An aggregator captures and organizes the feeds to simplify the user's reading experience.

Flipboard: It gathers content from social networks, news publications and blogs. Then the app displays stories, articles, blog posts, videos and other pieces of content in a magazine-like format. The Flipboard app is available on multiple operating systems and devices, including smartphones and tablets.

5. Blogging and Publishing Networks

These social media networks give you a place to publish your thoughts on your job, current events, hobbies and more. You can enjoy many of the benefits of having your own blog without having to host it on your own website. You can also attract new readers from the pool of people who visit the network looking for interesting content. Consider writing blog posts about how to use your product in creative ways or post news about your industry to drive more traffic to your account. Examples of blogging and publishing networks:

WordPress: WordPress is built on PHP, a general-purpose scripting language that meets web development needs. PHP is especially useful to create content management systems like WordPress because it enables interaction with a database and data fetching, outputting it for the user as HTML

Tumblr: The service allows users to post multimedia and other content to a short-form blog. Users can follow other users' blogs. Bloggers can also make their blogs private. For bloggers, many of the website's features are accessed from a "dashboard" interface. As of March 2023, Tumblr hosts more than 572 million blogs.

6. Consumer Review Networks

These sites display customers' reviews of businesses, giving users a full perspective of the type of services and products offered and the overall satisfaction rate. Customer reviews can help you identify any common problems that many people share and allow you to improve their experiences over time. Promoting positive reviews and thoughtfully handling negative ones can make your business more popular and boost brand awareness. Examples of consumer review networks:

TripAdvisor: It is an American company that operates online travel agencies, comparison shopping websites, and mobile apps with user-generated content.

Yelp: It is a crowd-sourced local business review and social networking site. The site has pages devoted to individual locations, such as restaurants or schools, where Yelp users can submit a review of their products or services using a one to five stars rating scale. Businesses can update contact information, hours, and other basic listing information or add special deals. In addition to writing reviews, users can react to reviews, plan events, or discuss their personal lives.

7. Interest-based Networks

Use these specialized networks to share your hobbies and unique interests with others. Sites and apps related to your industry can help you network by shared interest as well. For example, an interest-based site could allow people to discuss their favourite books and get recommendations about what to read next. Authors could create profile pages to promote their work and answer questions from readers. Examples of interest-based networks:

Strava: It incorporates social media features which allow users to post their exercises to followers. Alongside a GPS map of their exercise users can also post pictures and videos. Followers can then comment on posts and give 'kudos' in the form of a like button. Beacon is a feature that allows Strava users to share their location in real time with anyone they choose to, and nominate others as a safety contact for their workout. Other premium features include access to custom route-building tools and access to map segment leaderboards.

Goodreads: It is an American social cataloging website and a subsidiary of Amazon that allows individuals to search its database of books, annotations, quotes, and reviews. Users can sign up and register books to generate library catalogues and reading lists. They can also create their own groups of book suggestions, surveys, polls, blogs, and discussions.

8. Video Hosting Platforms

Video hosting platforms give independent filmmakers, journalists and other creators a way for their audiences to stream videos quickly and easily. Brands can use paid ads to reach new customers, they can ask influencers to use and talk about their products or they can film their own video content. Examples of video hosting platforms:

YouTube: YouTube is a website designed for sharing video. YouTube operates as one of Google's subsidiaries. YouTube allows users to upload, view, rate, share, add to playlists, report, comment on videos, and subscribe to other users. It offers a wide variety of user-generated and corporate media videos.

Vimeo: Vimeo is a video sharing platform that includes features such as live-streaming and customization. The platform is ad-free, and instead gains revenue by providing subscription plans for businesses and content creators and offering software as a service (SaaS). These services include video creation, editing, broadcasting tools and connecting with clients. The bottom line is that Vimeo allows you to create high quality, professional videos and reach audiences worldwide.

Social media posting guidelines for businesses give a rundown of the do's and don'ts on social media

The "do's and don'ts" format is perfect for listing out things super clearly, so start your social media guideline with that. Here's a good starting point:

- Do report any instance of harassment and bullying that you've experienced.
- Don't engage with trolls and bad actors on your own without consulting higher-ups.
- Do list your employer in your social media bio (make sure to specify that it's optional).
- Don't engage in flame wars with competitors, both direct and indirect, customers, followers, trolls, or any member of the company's social media audience.

- Do express your own opinion on social media. If the bio mentions the employer, state clearly that the opinions expressed are your own.
- Do share company posts, updates, events, and stories.
- Don't share company secrets. This can include but not be limited to, upcoming features, marketing campaigns that are still in the works, financial information, or any matters that could be considered internal.
- Do report any potential social media-related crisis.
- Don't comment, engage or get involved in legal matters related to the company.

Guidelines for Engaging Audience through Social Media

- **Identify your ideal outlets**: A great way to plan and begin a social campaign is to figure out where to run them. WebiMax, an online reputation management company, can evaluate website and, using the data it pulls, suggests the social media outlets that would be most beneficial for the company to focus on.
- **Knowing the Audience:** Understand your audience demographics, interests, and behaviours to tailor content that resonates with them.
- **Consistent Branding:** Maintain consistent branding across different social media platforms. Use a recognizable profile picture, cover photo, and cohesive messaging.
- **Compelling Content:** Create high-quality, valuable, and diverse content that educates, entertains, or solves problems for your audience. Mix formats like videos, images, infographics, polls, and stories.
- **Engage and Respond:** Actively engage with your audience by responding to comments, messages, and mentions. Encourage conversations, ask questions, and express genuine interest in their opinions.
- **Use Hashtags Strategically**: Employ relevant and trending hashtags to expand your reach and join relevant conversations. But avoid overusing them.
- **Timing is Key:** Post content at optimal times when your audience is most active. Use social media analytics to identify peak engagement periods.
- **Encourage User-Generated Content:** Encourage your audience to create and share content related to your brand. Run contests, challenges, or campaigns that involve user participation.

- **Live Videos and Stories:** Use live videos or stories to give a behind-the-scenes look, host Q&A sessions, product demonstrations, or share real-time updates. They create a sense of immediacy and authenticity.
- **Influencer Collaborations:** Partner with influencers or industry experts to reach a broader audience and leverage their credibility.
- **Calls-to-Action (CTAs):** Include clear CTAs in your posts to guide your audience on what actions to take next—whether it's visiting your website, subscribing, or sharing the content.
- **Community Building:** Foster a sense of community among your followers. Encourage them to interact with each other, share experiences, and support one another.
- **Monitor and Analyze:** Track metrics and analytics to understand what content performs best and adjust your strategy accordingly. Platforms often offer insights into reach, engagement, and audience demographics.
- **Adapt and Experiment:** Social media trends evolve rapidly. Experiment with new features, formats, and trends to keep your content fresh and engaging.
- **Be Authentic:** Show the human side of your brand. Be authentic, transparent, and relatable to establish genuine connections with your audience.
- **Stay Active**: Consistency is key. Maintain an active presence by regularly posting and engaging with your audience.

8

e-Governance

Boppana Jagadeeswari

College of Agriculture, Rajendranagar
Professor Jayashankar Telangana State Agricultural University, Hyderabad

e-Governance can be defined as the application of information and communication technology (ICT) for providing government services, exchange of information, transactions and integration of previously existing services and information portals. The "e" in e-Governance stands for 'electronic'.

e-Governance refers to the use of Information and Communication Technology (ICT), particularly web-based applications, to provide access to and deliver information/service to the public, businesses, other agencies and governmental entities faster, cheaper, easier and more efficiently.

The Council of **Europe** referred to e-governance as: "The use of electronic technologies in three areas of public action

1. Relations between the public authorities and civil society
2. The functioning of the public authorities at all stages of the democratic process (electronic democracy)
3. The provision of public services (electronic public services)

Reasons for Opting for e-Governance

- Governance per se has become very complex
- Increase in citizens' expectations from the government

Different Connotations of e-Governance

e-Administration: The use of ICTs to modernize the state; the creation of data repositories for Management Information System (MIS) and computerization of records (land, health etc).

e-Services: The emphasis here is to bring the state closer to the citizens. For Example: The provision of online services.

e-Governance: The use of IT to improve the ability of the government to address the needs of society. It includes the publishing of policy and program-related information to transact with citizens. It extends beyond the provision of online services and covers the use of IT for strategic planning and reaching the development goals of the government.

e-Democracy: The use of IT to facilitate the ability of all sections of society to participate in the governance of the state. Emphasis is on bringing transparency, accountability, and participation of people. It includes online disclosures of policies, online grievance redressal, e-referendums etc.

Origin

e-Governance originated in India during the 1970s with a focus on in-house government applications in the areas of defense, economic monitoring, planning and deployment of ICT to manage data-intensive functions related to elections, census, tax administration etc. Hence e-governance is basically a move towards SMART governance implying: simple, moral, accountable, responsive and transparent governance/objectives

- **Simple** — implies simplification of rules and regulations of the government and avoiding complex processes with the application of ICTs and therefore, providing a user-friendly government.
- **Moral** — meaning the emergence of a new system in the administrative and political machinery with technology interventions to improve the efficiency of various government agencies.
- **Accountable** — develop effective information management systems and other performance measurement mechanisms to ensure the accountability of public service functionaries.
- **Responsive** — Speed up processes by streamlining them, hence making the system more responsive.
- **Transparent** — providing information in the public domain like websites or various portals hence making functions and processes of the government transparent.

The latest e-Governance projects are e-kranti, Digi locker, darpan and PRAGATI (Pro-Active Governance and Timely Implementation) by Ministry of Electronics and Information Technology.

The initial initiatives taken in India for e-governance are as follows

- The establishment of the Department of Electronics in 1970 was the first major step towards e-governance in India as it brought 'information' and its communication to focus.
- National Informatics Centre (NIC) established in 1977, launched the District Information System program to computerize all district offices in the country.
- The main thrust for e-governance was provided by the launching of NICNET in 1987 – the national satellite-based computer network.
- The National Task Force on Information Technology and Software Development was established in 1998.
- The Ministry of Information Technology was created at the centre in 1999.
- The 12-point agenda has been listed for e-Governance for the execution in all the central ministries and departments.
- The Information Technology Act (2000) was enacted and was amended in 2008.
- The very first National Conference of States IT Ministers was organized in the year 2000, for implementing the Common Actions Plan to promote Information Technology in India
- The government set up NISG (National Institute for Smart Government)
- The state governments launched e-Governance projects like e-Seva, Bhoomi, and so on.
- The National e-Governance Plan (NeGP) was launched on 2006 which consists of 8 support components and 31 Mission Mode Projects (MMPs)
- The National Policy on Information Technology (NPIT) was acquired in 2012.

Objectives

- Better service delivery to citizens.
- Ushering in transparency and accountability.
- Empowering people through information.

- Improve efficiency within Government i.e., between centre-state or inter-states.
- Improve interface with business and industry.

Pillars of e-Governance

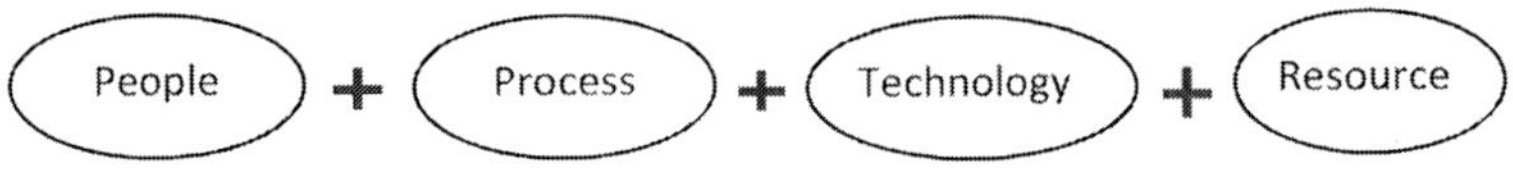

Types of Interaction in e-Governance

A. G2G (Government to Government)

- G2G allows seamless interaction between various government institutions.
- Government to Government interaction can be between various departments and agencies within government or between two governmental organisations like the union and state governments or between state governments.
- The primary aim of G2G is to increase efficiency, performance, and output

B. G2C (Government to Citizen)

- It is the interaction between the government and the citizens.
- G2C entitles citizens to benefit from the systemic delivery of a large range of public services.
- Expands the accessibility and availability of government services and improves the quality of services
- The primary aim of G2C is to build a citizen-friendly government.

C. G2B (Government to Business)

- The primary objective of G2B is to cut strict regulations which will save time and reduce operational costs creating a more transparent business environment when dealing with the government.
- It helps in services such as licensing, procurement, permits, and revenue collection

D. G2E (Government to Employees)

- Government to Employees interaction is between the government and its employees.

- ICT (Information and Communications Technology) tools help in making these interactions fast and efficient and thus increasing the satisfaction levels of employees.

Advantages of e-Governance

- Improves delivery and efficiency of government services
- Improved government interactions with business and industry
- Citizen empowerment through access to information
- More efficient government management
- Less corruption in the administration
- Increased transparency in administration
- Greater convenience to citizens and businesses
- Cost reductions and revenue growth
- Increased legitimacy of government
- Flattens organisational structure (less hierarchic)
- Reduces paperwork and red-tapism in the administrative process which results in better planning and coordination between different levels of government
- Improved relations between the public authorities and civil society
- Re-structuring of administrative processes

Stages of E-Governance

United Nations E-Readiness Survey defined below mentioned stages of E-governance:

1. **Emerging Presence:** The focus in this stage is at the online presence of basic & limited information which contains an official website along with a few web pages. There is not much clarity on the availability of the links to various ministries and departments.

2. **Enhanced Presence:** The public information like reports, newsletters, laws and policies is shared largely by the Government and it is also possible for the users to navigate within the records. The only limitation that lies is that of one-way communication as the information transfer is only from Government to citizens and not the other way round.

3. **Interactive Presence:** This marks the introduction of interactivity in the Government websites in the form of making downloadable forms available & applications for payment of bills, taxes, and license renewal.
4. **Transactional Presence:** The provisions such as applying for ID cards, license renewals, birth certificates, passports, and allowing the citizen to submit forms and applications online in a never-ending manner makes the ideal functioning of two-way interaction between the Government and citizens very much possible.
5. **Networked Presence:** It is interpreted by an amalgamation of G2C, G2G, and G2B interactions. The citizen participation is encouraged to realise online participatory decision-making with the Government which helps in establishing a two-way open dialogue within the society.

E-Governance four stage evolution

- **Computerization:** Personal computers were available in many government offices. Many departments of government started using personal computers and programmes like word processing, data processing, etc.
- **Networking:** In this stage, many government offices were interconnected through a network. This facilitated the inter-departmental network for information sharing and flow of data.
- **Online presence:** With the increasing network capabilities of government offices, the need was felt to have an online presence of government departments. Websites of government departments came into existence. These websites provided basic information to the citizens such as reports, surveys, schemes, etc.
- **Online interactivity:** The two-way communication was established in this stage where people could send their feedback to the government through an online portal. This changed the role of citizens merely from the recipient of services to the active involvement of citizens in governance.

National policies on e-governance

The National e-Governance Plan (NeGP)

- The National e-Governance Plan (NeGP) provides a holistic view of e-Governance initiatives across the country.

- Around this idea, a massive countrywide infrastructure reaching down to the remotest of villages is evolving, and large-scale digitization of records is taking place to enable easy, reliable access to the internet.
- The Government has proposed to implement "e-Kranti: National e-Governance Plan (NeGP) 2.0" under the Digital India programme.

e-Kranti – Electronic Delivery of Services

- e-Kranti is an essential pillar of the Digital India initiative.
- Considering the critical need for e-Governance, mobile governance and good governance in the country, the approach and key components of e-Kranti have been approved by the government.
- The e-Kranti framework addresses the electronic delivery of services through a portfolio of mission mode projects that cut across several government departments.

Objectives of e-Kranti

The main aims of the initiative are to

- Redefine NeGP with transformational and outcome-oriented e-Governance initiatives
- Enhance the portfolio of citizen-centric services
- Ensure optimum usage of core Information & Communication Technology (ICT)
- Promote rapid replication and integration of e-Governance applications
- Leverage emerging technologies
- Make use of more agile implementation models

S.No.	Program	Details
1.	Bhoomi Project (Karnataka): Online Delivery of Land Records	• Bhoomi is a self-sustainable e-Governance project for the computerized delivery of 20 million rural land records to 6.7 million farmers of Karnataka.
2.	KHAJANE (Karnataka): End-to-end automation of Government Treasury System	• 'Government-to-government (G2G) e-Government initiative of the Karnataka state government. • It has been implemented mainly to eliminate systemic deficiencies in the manual treasury system and for the efficient management of state finances.

S.No.	Program	Details
3.	e-Seva (Andhra Pradesh):	• Designed to provide 'Government to Citizen' and 'e-Business to Citizen' services. • All the services are delivered online to consumers / citizens by connecting them to the respective government departments and providing online information at the point of service delivery. • The project has become very popular among the citizens especially for the payment of utility bills
4.	e-Courts:	• Launched by the Department of Justice, Ministry of Law and Justice. • The Mission Mode Project (MMP) aims at utilizing technology for improved provisioning of judicial services to citizens.
5.	e- District:	• Launched by the Department of Information Technology. • The MMP aims at delivery of high volume, citizen-centric services at the District level such as the issue of birth/ death certificate, income and caste certificates, old age and widow pension, etc.
6.	MCA21:	• Launched by the Ministry of Corporate Affairs. • The project aims to provide electronic services to the Companies registered under the Companies Act. • Various online facilities offered includes allocation and change of name, incorporation, online payment of registration charges, change in address of registered office, viewing of public records and other related services.
7.	e-Office	• Launched by the Department of Administrative Reforms & Public Grievances. • The MMP aims at significantly improving the operational efficiency of the Government by transitioning to a "Less Paper Office".

Digital India Programme

The Ministry of Electronics and Information Technology (MeitY), Government of India launched the 'Digital India' programme with the vision to transform India into a digitally empowered society and knowledge-based economy by ensuring digital access, digital inclusion, digital empowerment and bridging the digital divide. In summary, our mission is to ensure that the digital technologies improve the life of every citizen; expand India's digital economy, create investment & employment opportunities and global digital technological capabilities in the country.

Digital India has dramatically reduced distance between Government and citizens significantly. Further, Digital India has also helped in delivery of substantial services directly to the beneficiary in a transparent and corruption free manner. India has become one of the pre-eminent nations of the world to use technology to transform the lives of citizens. Digital India is an umbrella programme that covers multiple projects of various Central Ministries/ Departments and States/UTs.

S.No.	Program	Details
1.	Common Services Centres	• CSCs are offering government and business services in digital mode in rural areas through Village Level Entrepreneurs (VLEs). Over 400 digital services are being offered by these CSCs. • So far, 5.31 Lakh CSCs are functional (including urban & rural areas) across the country, out of which, 4.20 Lakh CSCs are functional at Gram Panchayat level.
2.	Unified Mobile Application for New-age Governance (UMANG)	• It is for providing government services to citizen through mobile. More than 1,570 government services and over 22,000 bill payment services are made available at UMANG.
3.	PRAGATI	• A system that aims at establishing e-accountability and implementing e-transparency
4.	Digi-Locker	• It is facilitating paperless availability of public documents. Digital Locker has more than 11.7 crore users and more than 532 crore documents are made available through Digi-Locker from 2,167 issuer organisations.
5.	Unified Payment Interface (UPI)	• It is the leading digital payment platform. It is integrated with 330 banks and facilitated over 586 crore monthly transactions worth over Rs 10 lakh crore has been facilitated for the month of June, 2022.
6.	CO-WIN	• It is an open platform for management of registration, appointment scheduling & managing vaccination certificates for Covid-19. More than 203 crore vaccination doses and 110 crore registrations have been facilitated by co-win.
7.	MyGov	• It is a citizen engagement platform that is developed to facilitate participatory governance. More than 2.48 crore users are actively using MyGov.
8.	Meri Pehchaan	• National Single Sign-on platform called Meri Pehchaan has been launched in July 2022 to facilitate / provide citizens ease of access to government portals
9.	My Scheme	• This platform has been launched in July 2022 to facilitate citizens to avail eligibility-based services.
10.	Direct Benefit Transfer	• 315 Schemes across 53 Ministries are offering Aadhaar enabled direct benefit transfer to citizens. So far, Rs 24.3 lakh crore has been disbursed through DBT platform.
11.	Diksha	• Diksha is a national level educational platform that helps students and teachers to participate, contribute and leverage a common platform to achieve learning goals at scale for the country. As on 27th July 2022, **7,633** courses are available and more than 15 crore enrolments have been done.

Challenges of National policies on E-Governance

Infrastructure

- Lack of basic infrastructural facilities like electricity, internet, etc.
- Initiatives like **Bharat-Net** and **Sau-bhagyaa** are steps taken in this regard.

Cost

- e-Governance measures are costly affairs and require huge public expenditure.
- In developing countries like India, the cost of projects is one of the major impediments in the implementation of e-Governance initiatives.

Privacy and Security-

- Recent spark in data leak cases has threatened the peoples' faith in e-governance.
- Therefore, the implementation of e-governance projects must have security standards and protocols for safeguarding the interest of all classes of masses.

Digital Divide

- Huge gap between users and non-users of e-govt. services.
- The digital divide takes form in rich-poor, male-female, urban-rural etc segments of the population.
- The gap needs to be narrowed down, then only the benefits of e-governance would be utilized equally.

National e-Agricultural Policy/ Strategies/ Guidelines

E-agriculture involves designing, developing and applying innovative ways to use information and communication technologies (ICTs), including digital technologies - in the rural domain, with a primary focus on agriculture, including fisheries, forestry and livestock.

The aim is to boost agricultural and rural development by improving access to valuable information that can help people whose livelihoods depend on agriculture to make the best possible decisions and use the resources available in the most productive and sustainable manner.

The Key Objectives of the Project Include

- Bringing farmer centricity & service orientation to the programs
- Enhancing reach & impact of extension services
- Improving access of farmers to information & services throughout crop cycle
- Building upon, enhancing & integrating the existing ICT initiatives of Centre, and States
- Enhancing efficiency & effectiveness of programs through process redesign
- More effective management of schemes of DAC
- Promoting a common framework across states

The Need for a National e-agriculture Strategy

The national e-agriculture strategy document provides an essential framework for developing or revitalizing a country's e-agriculture strategy in alignment with agricultural goals and priorities. It can be used equally by countries just setting out and those which have already invested significantly in e-agriculture. This latter group includes countries now seeking to build on promising results from pilot initiatives, to establish foundations for scaling up e-agriculture projects, or to update current strategies to reflect changing economic circumstances. Whatever the starting point, e-agriculture efforts can be strengthened, accelerated or aligned through a national strategic planning process.

National policies on e-Agriculture

S.No.	Program	Details
1.	National Agriculture Market (e-NAM)	Government of India has launched National Agriculture Market (e-NAM) Scheme with the objective of creating online transparent competitive bidding system to facilitate farmers with remunerative prices for their produce. More than 1.73 crore farmers & 2.26 lakh traders have been registered on e-NAM platform. Also, 1000 mandis of 18 States and 3 UTs have been integrated with e-NAM platform
2.	M-KISAN	m-Kisan Portal (www.mkisan.gov.in) for sending advisories on various crop related matters to the registered farmers through SMSs. In m-kisan more than 5.13 crore farmers are registered for receiving crop advisories through SMS. More than 2,462 crore mobile based advisories have been sent to farmers to assist them in their farming activities.

S.No.	Program	Details
3.	One Stop Window-Farmers Portal (www.farmer.gov.in)	It is for dissemination of information on various agricultural related matter including, seeds variety, Storage Godown, Pests and plant diseases, Best Agricultural Practices, Watershed, Mandi details etc.
4.	Soil Health Card	It provides soil related information to facilitate farmers in farming activities. More than 22 crore soil health cards have been printed and dispatched to farmers
5.	Mobile based advisory system for agriculture & Horticulture (M4AGRI)	It is mobile based advisory system for agriculture and horticulture. It has been implemented in the North-East States namely Tripura, Mizoram, Manipur, Meghalaya, Sikkim, and Arunachal Pradesh.
6.	Pradhan Mantri Fasal Bima Yojana (PMFBY)	PMFBY is a crop insurance scheme that leverages technology for quick claim settlement. It incorporates remote sensing, satellite imagery, and smartphones to assess crop damage and provide financial support to farmers.
7.	Kisan Credit Card (KCC)	KCC is a government scheme that provides farmers with a credit card to meet their agricultural credit requirements. The KCC scheme has been digitized to simplify the application process and enable online transactions.
8.	Rashtriya Krishi Vikas Yojana (RKVY)	RKVY is a centrally sponsored scheme that promotes the use of technology in agriculture. It supports projects related to the development of e-marketing, e-extension services, and other digital initiatives to enhance farm productivity.
9.	Agri-Tech Infrastructure Fund (ATIF)	The ATIF was announced in the Union Budget 2021-22 to strengthen the e-agriculture ecosystem. It aims to provide financial assistance for the development of agricultural infrastructure, including e-marketing platforms, agri-tech startups, and innovative solutions.

Language Technology and It's Application under e-Governance

Language technology refers to the use of computational methods and technologies to analyse, understand, generate, and manipulate human language. It encompasses various areas such as natural language processing (NLP), speech recognition, machine translation, text-to-speech synthesis, sentiment analysis, and information retrieval.

Under e-governance, language technology plays a crucial role in facilitating communication and interaction between citizens and government entities. Here are some applications of language technology in e-governance:

a) **Machine Translation**: Language technology enables the translation of government information and services into multiple languages. This helps in reaching out to citizens who speak different languages and ensuring inclusivity and accessibility.

b) **Natural Language Processing:** NLP techniques allow the government to process and understand vast amounts of textual data, such as citizen feedback, complaints, and public opinions. NLP can be used for sentiment analysis, information extraction, and topic modeling, enabling governments to gauge public sentiment and make informed decisions.

c) **Speech Recognition:** Speech recognition technology enables the conversion of spoken language into written text. It can be used in interactive voice response (IVR) systems to automate customer service and handle citizen queries efficiently.

d) **Text-to-Speech Synthesis**: Text-to-speech technology can convert written information into spoken language, facilitating accessibility for visuallyz impaired citizens. Government documents, notifications, and other important information can be made available in audio formats.

e) **Information Retrieval:** Language technology aids in efficient retrieval and search of government information. Citizens can easily access relevant documents, policies, laws, and procedures through search engines and chatbots powered by NLP techniques.

f) **Chatbots and Virtual Assistants:** Language technology enables the development of chatbots and virtual assistants that can engage with citizens, answer frequently asked questions, provide guidance on government services, and assist in filling out forms or applications.

g) **Multilingual Call Centers:** Language technology can enhance the functionality of call centers by providing multilingual support. Citizens can communicate with government representatives in their preferred language, ensuring effective communication and better service delivery.

9

e-Learning

Sharmistha Swayamprava

Department of Agricultural Extension, University of Agricultural Sciences Dharwad, Karnataka

---

e-Learning

It is the concept of learning which is conducted via electronic media. This is usually via the Internet but can also be offline with a CD-Rom or DVD. Examples of e-Learning in icar: e krishi siksha, e-agri diksha web education channel of icar and virtual classroom of icar.

Advantages

- It promotes active and independent learning
- An efficient way of delivering courses as the resources are available from anywhere and at any time
- Students can interact with their peers from all around the world through group discussions and private chats
- The studying material can be accessed an unlimited number of times.
- Reduces cost and time
- E-learning can be carried out anywhere without strict time boundations it leads to a more flexible environment for students.
- In e-Learning, the people have the flexibility to choose course/ training obtain their own requirement of knowledge.

Initiatives of e-Learning

1. e-Krishi shiksha

Under Learning and Capacity Building program of NAIP, several UG level interactive & multimedia e-Courseware contents in seven discipline viz. Agricultural Science, Fisheries Science etc. have been developed at SAUs and other organisations.

2. Farmers e-World

Most of the SAUs and ICAR institutes are providing advisory support to the farmers in terms of short-term training programmes on agriculture, horticulture, home science, fisheries, dairy, veterinary and animal husbandry etc.

3. AEC e-Learning

The Department of Agricultural Education and Communication's online Master of Science option was developed to provide agricultural educators, extension agents, and leaders an opportunity to continue their education while working by attending graduate school online. The Master of Science degree is a six-semester program tailored to meet the needs of busy professionals who are looking for a distance degree program that is compatible with their current work.

4. Gender in Agriculture E-Learning Course

It is the product of a collaboration between the World Bank and Michigan State University and is based on the Gender in Agriculture Sourcebook (2009), result of a fruitful partnership of the World Bank, FAO. This online course provides answers across different sub-sectors to the question.

M-learning or mobile learning

It is "learning across multiple contexts, through social and content interactions, using personal electronic devices" or Mobile learning(m-learning) is learning via the Internet or network using personal mobile devices, such as tablets and smartphones to obtain learning materials through mobile apps, social interactions and inline educational hubs.

E.g. AgMoocs by IIT Kanpur, Icar e learning portal Krishi siksha, Matya setu (icar-Cifa Virtual learning app on fresh water aquaculture contains video lectures).

e.g.: matysa setu, Rice knowledge management portal m-learning (RKMP m-learning developed by CDAC Hyderabad.

Massive Open Online Course (MOOC)

A massive open online course (MOOC) is a model for delivering learning content online to any person who wants to take a course, with no limit on attendance.

In addition to traditional course materials such as filmed lectures, readings, and problem sets, many MOOCs provide interactive user forums to support community interactions among students, professors, and teaching assistants

(TAs). MOOCs are a recent and widely researched development in distance education. Most MOOCs are structured similar to traditional online higher education courses in which students watch lectures, read assigned material, participate in online discussions and forums, and complete quizzes and tests on the course material. MOOCs are typically provided by higher education institutions, often in partnership with "organizers" such as Coursera, edX, and Udacity.

There are 2 types of MOOC

A. **c-MOOC:** instructional design approaches attempt to connect learners to each other to answer questions and/or collaborate on joint projects. This may include emphasizing collaborative development of the MOOC.

B. **x-MOOC:** shares more traditional course structure typically with a clearly specified syllabus of recorded lectures and self-test problems. The instructor is the expert provider of knowledge, and student interactions are usually limited to asking for assistance and advising each other on difficult points.

Principles

- Content: The content and design should be need-based and user-centric.
- Delivery mechanism: The business and pricing model, mode of delivery (text, interactive voice response, call, pictures, videos, etc.), and choice of application-based versus normal access
- Reach and interaction: Rigorous awareness-raising programmes should be conducted to increase reach, and the services should be interactive to ensure clients' needs are being met.
- Communication, not just advisory: encourage increased dialogue between the stakeholders in agricultural innovation systems rather than providing farmers with information.
- Sustainability: Both financial and infrastructural sustainability can be ensured by using a profit-based model of information delivery.
- Integration of technology: Different formats such as web portals, videos, voice, pictures and animations, etc. can be easily accessed from mobile phones, thus making integration of technology easier and efficient, and increasing the scope of m-Extension.
- Reassessment vs development: Often it is better to build on existing services rather than coming up with new ones.

- Associated services: Infrastructure like roads, electricity, education, market and credit access, and so on are also required.

Advantages

1. Accessibility: MOOCs offer education to a global audience, allowing people from different parts of the world to access courses from prestigious institutions.
2. Flexibility: Learners can access course materials at their convenience, allowing them to study at their own pace and schedule, making education more accessible to working professionals and students with busy lifestyles.
3. Cost-Effective: Many MOOCs are free or significantly cheaper than traditional education, reducing barriers to quality education.
4. Diverse Course Offerings: MOOC platforms host a wide variety of courses covering diverse subjects, allowing learners to explore various fields of interest.
5. Interactive Learning: Some MOOCs incorporate interactive elements like quizzes, assignments, and discussion forums, fostering engagement and interaction among learners.

Limitations

1. Lack of Personalization: MOOCs may lack personalized interaction with instructors, limiting the ability to ask questions and receive immediate feedback compared to traditional classroom settings.
2. Low Completion Rates: A significant number of enrolled learners do not complete MOOCs. Factors like lack of motivation, busy schedules, or the absence of accountability contribute to this.
3. Limited Credential Value: While some MOOCs offer certificates upon completion, the recognition and value of these credentials vary across industries and employers. They might not hold the same weight as traditional degrees or certifications.
4. Technology and Access Constraints: Access to MOOCs relies on stable internet connections and adequate technological resources, which might not be universally available, especially in less developed regions.
5. Quality and Credibility: The quality of MOOCs can vary significantly, and not all courses offered on MOOC platforms maintain the same level of credibility or academic rigor as traditional educational institutions.

6. Lack of Hands-On Experience: Some subjects, especially those requiring hands-on practical training or laboratory work, might be challenging to teach effectively through MOOCs.
7. MOOCs continue to evolve, addressing some limitations through innovations in teaching methods, better interactive elements, and improved certification recognition. However, these challenges persist and influence their effectiveness for certain types of learners and subjects.

10

Multimedia

Yelasani Ishwarya

Agricultural Extension, School of Social Sciences
College of Post Graduate Studies in Agricultural Sciences, Umaim
CAU, Impal, Manipur

Multimedia refers to the integration of various forms of media, including text, audio, video, graphics, and animations, to convey information or entertainment. It's a powerful tool used in various fields due to its ability to engage multiple senses simultaneously.

Aspects of Multimedia

- Text: Written content forms the basis of multimedia, providing information, context, and explanations.
- Audio: Sound elements, such as music, narration, or sound effects, enhance the overall experience, making content more engaging and informative.
- Video: Moving images and footage bring visual content to life, allowing for storytelling, demonstrations, or presentations in a dynamic format.
- Graphics and Images: Visual elements, including photos, illustrations, charts, and graphs, aid in explaining complex concepts or adding visual appeal to content.
- Animations: Moving graphics or illustrations help illustrate processes, explain concepts, or entertain users.

Applications of Multimedia

Education: Multimedia is extensively used in educational settings, enhancing learning experiences through interactive lessons, video lectures, simulations, and online courses.

Entertainment: In movies, video games, music videos, and other forms of entertainment, multimedia creates immersive and engaging experiences for audiences.

Advertising and Marketing: Multimedia elements are vital in advertising campaigns, utilizing audio-visual content to attract and engage consumers.

Digital Media and Journalism: News websites, blogs, and online publications use multimedia to present information, incorporating videos, images, and interactive graphics to tell stories.

Business Presentations: Multimedia aids in creating compelling presentations by integrating various media formats to convey messages effectively.

Art and Design: Multimedia tools are used in artistic expressions, digital art, animation, and graphic design to create visually appealing content.

Advantages of Multimedia

- Enhanced Engagement: It captures attention more effectively than text-only content.
- Improved Learning: Multimedia aids in better comprehension and retention of information.
- Versatility: It allows for diverse forms of expression and communication.
- Creative Expression: Enables artists and creators to explore innovative ways of presenting ideas.

Challenges of Multimedia

- Technical Complexity: Creating multimedia content may require specialized software and skills.
- Compatibility: Different devices and platforms might interpret multimedia content differently.
- Accessibility: Not all users have equal access to multimedia content due to disabilities or technological limitations.
- Multimedia continues to evolve, shaping how information is shared, consumed, and understood across various domains.

Basic Principles of Multimedia Learning

Coherence Principle – People learn more deeply from a multimedia message when extraneous material such as words, pictures and sounds is excluded rather than included.

- The rationale for the coherence principle is that people are better able to focus on the essential material if we eliminate extraneous material that could distract them.
- Given that learning is an active process, these extraneous details may interfere with learners' construction of mental models to represent the material.

To address this principle

- Include only graphics, text, and narration that support learning goals (i.e., don't use decorative images or supplemental materials).
- Don't use background music.
- Use simple visuals (as opposed to realistic or detailed visuals).

1. **Signaling Principle** – People learn better when cues that highlight the organization of the essential material are added.
2. **Redundancy Principle** – People learn better from graphics and narration than from graphics, narration and on-screen text.
3. **Spatial Contiguity Principle** – People learn better when corresponding words and pictures are presented near rather than far from each other on the page or screen.
4. **Temporal Contiguity Principle** – People learn better when corresponding words and pictures are presented simultaneously rather than successively.
5. **Segmenting Principle** – People learn better from a multimedia lesson is presented in user-paced segments rather than as a continuous unit.
6. **Pre-training Principle** – People learn better from a multimedia lesson when they know the names and characteristics of the main concepts.
7. **Modality Principle** – People learn better from graphics and narrations than from animation and on-screen text.
8. **Multimedia Principle** – People learn better from words and pictures than from words alone.
9. **Personalization Principle** – People learn better from multimedia lessons when words are in conversational style rather than formal style.
10. **Voice Principle** – People learn better when the narration in multimedia lessons is spoken in a friendly human voice rather than a machine voice.

11. **Image Principle** – People do not necessarily learn better from a multimedia lesson when the speaker's image is added to the screen.

The Split-attention Principle

Split-attention Principle states that when designing instruction, including multimedia instruction, it is important to avoid formats that require learners to split their attention between, mentally integrate and multiple sources of information. According to this principle, words should be presented auditorily rather than visually.

Example- When a student reads a story and encounters an unfamiliar word, given a separate glossary, the student leaves the text and turns to the vocabulary list. Learner temporarily stores its meaning and then reverts to the text and tries to incorporate the word meaning into the passage.

The Modality principle

People learn more deeply from a multimedia message when the words are spoken rather than printed. The dual-channel and limited-capacity assumptions lead in part to the modality principle, which recommends that instructors use narration instead of on-screen text when pictures are present.

If multimedia messages contain pictures and on-screen text, the combination may overwhelm learners' visual channels. Instead, instructors should only speak words (rather than include them on-screen), which spreads the load across both the visual and the verbal channels (also known as "modality offloading").

To address this principle: During a narrated presentation with graphics, avoid using on-screen text, unless it:

- Lists key steps
- Provides directions
- Provides references
- Presents important information to non-native English speakers

The Redundancy Principle

"People learn better from graphics and narration than some graphics, narration, and printed text." Many multimedia presentations involve a combination of spoken words, graphics, and on-screen text.

However, the redundancy principle suggests that multimedia messages are most effective when learners encounter just spoken words and graphics. When instructors include text on-screen, they risk overwhelming their learners' visual channels with both pictures and words, and inadvertently direct their cognitive processes to resolving differences between the spoken text and the printed text.

To address this principle

- When delivering a narrated presentation, use either graphics or text, but not both.
- Minimize the use of text during a narrated presentation.

The Signaling Principle

People learn more deeply from a multimedia message when cues are added that highlight the organization of the essential material.

The rationale for the signaling principle is that people will learn more efficiently is the lesson is designed to call their attention to the important material in the lesson. Particularly when multiple pieces of information are on-screen, learners need to know what to pay attention to, where they are in the presentation, and how to integrate the information to construct their own mental models.

To address this principle

- Use arrows, highlighting, and other signals to draw attention to important information.

The Segmenting Principle

"People learn better when a multimedia message is presented in user-paced segments rather than as a continuous unit." Mayer's experiments determined that when students had the ability to control the pace of the lesson, they performed better on recall and transfer tests.

Thus, the segmenting principle has two implications:

(a) users should have control over the pace of the multimedia lesson, and

(b) instructors should chunk material appropriately to allow for adequate processing on each slide or screen.

To address this principle

- Allow users to control the pace of the lesson, such as speed controls or "next" buttons.
- Break down long segments of material into smaller pieces.

The Pre-Training Principle

"People learn more deeply from a multimedia message when they know the names and characteristics of the main concepts." The pre-training principle accordingly recommends that instructors define key terms or concepts before diving into descriptions of processes. Otherwise, students will be stuck trying to learn a process's component parts while also attempting to build a mental model of the process itself, which may hinder learning.

To address this principle

1. Define key terms (such as names, definitions, locations, and characteristics) before beginning a process-based presentation, either in a separate presentation, handout, or similar material.
2. Ensure people know how to use a tool (such as Excel) before asking them to perform learning activities within it.

The Personalization Principle

"People learn better from multimedia presentations when words are in conversational style rather than formal style." According to the personalization principle, having a more relaxed tone in an online class can actually positively impact learning. Thus, instructors should avoid stiff, academic language, and instead use more approachable colloquial language.

To address this principle

- Use contractions.
- Use first and second person ("I," "you," "we," "our," etc.).
- If using a script, try to make an extemporaneous-sounding performance.
- Use polite speech ("please," "you might like to," "let's," etc.).

The Voice embodiment Principle

"People learn better when narration is spoken in a human voice rather than in a machine voice." The voice principle is perhaps the oddest of the group, but it is still worthy of mention, particularly given the speed at which technology is developing. This principle suggests that narration is better done by a human than a computer. To address this principle: Include narration that's performed by a human rather than a computer.

Advanced principles of Multimedia Learning

1. **Guided -discovery principle-** People learn better when guidance is

incorporated into discovery-based multimedia environments. In this way instruction that explains principles and rules in a domain to a learner is created.

2. **Worked-out example principle-** People learn better when they receive worked-out examples in initial skill learning. The worked example principle is based on using solved examples that guide learners through a step by step process to solve a task or a problem to reduce cognitive load as they are learning a new concept.
3. **Collaboration principle-** People can learn better with collaborative online learning activities. Some examples of such activities may include students introducing themselves to each other online, reviewing each other's writing, and discussing content through online discussion forums.
4. **Self-explanation principle-** People learn better when they are encouraged to generate self-explanations during learning.
5. **Prior knowledge principle-** Instructional design principles that enhance multi-media learning for novices may hinder multimedia learning for more expert learners.
6. **Drawing principle** – This principle ask students to create drawings while reading text causes generative processing that leads to better learning outcomes. In drawing, students have to translate the verbal text information into a picture that represents spatial relationships among functional elements referred to in the text.
7. **Feedback principle** – The feedback principle states that novice students learn better with explanatory feedback than with corrective feedback alone. Explanatory feedback guides the learner in selecting the appropriate information and consequently reduces the amount of extraneous processing.
8. **Multiple representation principle-** Presenting words and pictures is more effective than processing words alone. Learners can gain deeper understanding when they abstract over multiple representations to achieve insight into the nature of the representations and the domain.
9. **Learner control principle-** The learner control principle suggests that giving learners to control over their instruction by allowing them to pace, sequence, and select information aids learning possess high levels of prior knowledge and is they receive additional instructional support

to orient themselves in the learning environment and to self-regulate their learning.

10. **Working memory principle-** This principle suggests that presenting information using both visual and auditory channels enhances learning and retention compared to using only one channel.

This principle takes advantage of dual coding and the modality effect to enhance encoding and retrieval from memory.

11

Artificial Intelligence

Md. Mubeena

Aricultural Extension, S.V. Agriculture College
Acharya N.G. Ranga Agricultural University, Tirupathi

Artificial intelligence is founded on the idea that human intelligence may be described in such a way that a computer can simply imitate it and carry out tasks ranging from simple to sophisticated. Artificial intelligence is assisting several agricultural sectors in increasing output and efficiency. In every industry, AI technologies are assisting in overcoming traditional hurdles.

AI intervention in agriculture is assisting farmers in increasing their farming efficiency while reducing harmful environmental impacts. The agriculture business has embraced AI with open arms in order to improve overall results. The way food is produced is changing as a result of artificial intelligence. Incorporating AI technology into agriculture aids in the control and management of any unwelcome natural occurrence.

Artificial intelligence is the simulation of human intelligence processes by machines, especially computer systems. Specific applications of AI include expert systems, natural language processing, speech recognition and machine vision.

The impact of artificial intelligence on agriculture in India

The World Economic Forum's Artificial Intelligence for Agriculture Innovation initiative aims to transform the agriculture sector in India by promoting the use of artificial intelligence (AI) and other technologies. Led by the Centre for the Fourth Industrial Revolution India and the Platform for Shaping the Future of Artificial Intelligence and Machine Learning, the initiative brings together government, academia and business representatives to collaborate on the development and implementation of innovative solutions in the agriculture sector.

What's the challenge to implementing AI for agriculture in India?

India is faced with the challenge of feeding a growing population while also addressing such risks as climate change, pandemics and supply chain disruptions. To address these challenges, the agricultural sector needs to become more agile and efficient. There are currently more than 1,000 agri-tech startups in India offering a range of tech-based solutions, including digital finance, micro-insurance, access to agricultural inputs, quality testing, traceability and market connect platforms. They have the potential to significantly contribute to improving productivity and sustainability, but fragmented technological infrastructure, high cost of operations, lack of access to data and limited technical expertise, hamper the scale of these technologies.

Advantages of AI

- Good at detail-oriented jobs. AI has proven to be as good or better than doctors at diagnosing certain cancers, including breast cancer and melanoma.
- Reduced time for data-heavy tasks. AI is widely used in data-heavy industries, including banking and securities, pharma and insurance, to reduce the time it takes to analyze big data sets. Financial services, for example, routinely use AI to process loan applications and detect fraud.
- Saves labor and increases productivity. An example here is the use of warehouse automation, which grew during the pandemic and is expected to increase with the integration of AI and machine learning.
- Delivers consistent results. The best AI translation tools deliver high levels of consistency, offering even small businesses the ability to reach customers in their native language.
- Can improve customer satisfaction through personalization. AI can personalize content, messaging, ads, recommendations and websites to individual customers.
- AI-powered virtual agents are always available. AI programs do not need to sleep or take breaks, providing 24/7 service.

Limitations of AI

- Expensive.
- Requires deep technical expertise.
- Limited supply of qualified workers to build AI tools.
- Reflects the biases of its training data, at scale.

- Lack of ability to generalize from one task to another.
- Eliminates human jobs, increasing unemployment rates.

IoT (Internet of things)

Since the coining of the term in 1999, the internet of things (IoT) has transformed from a mere vision to a palpable reality. This can be attributed to the extensive use of the Internet Protocol (IP), the rise of ubiquitous computing, and the continued advancement of data analytics, among other drivers of development. By 2020, it is estimated that there will be 20.4 billion devices connected to the IoT. Despite its continuing expansion, however, the IoT remains to some degree an obscure concept, something that's often referred to in abstract terms even as it provides manifest benefits.

The IoT can be described as an extension of the internet and other network connections to different sensors and devices — or "things" — affording even simple objects, such as lightbulbs, locks, and vents, a higher degree of computing and analytical capabilities.

In an agricultural context refers to the use of sensors, cameras and other devices to turn every element and action involved in farming into data. The aim of most agriculture IoT products is to enable farmers to use these insights to make operational decisions around planting, irrigating, harvesting and more. Interoperability is one of the key aspects of the IoT that contribute to its growing popularity. Connected or "smart" devices — as "things" in the IoT are often called — have the ability to gather and share data from their environments with other devices and networks. Through the analysis and processing of the data, devices can perform their functions with little or no need for human interaction.

Given the ever-increasing number of connected devices, the IoT continues its path of evolution, adding different layers to the data that is already being shared and processed, and giving rise to sophisticated algorithms that result in improved levels of automation. And because of the variety of "things" that can be connected to it, the IoT has enabled diverse applications for individual users and entire industries alike.

Major applications of IoT-based smart farming that are revolutionizing the agriculture sector

1. **Monitoring of farmland information with UAV:**Unmanned aerial vehicles (UAVs) are remote sensing autonomous vehicles that assist in the capture of photos and data about a specific location. The use of

unmanned aerial vehicles (UAVs) results in cheap operational costs in large-scale environmental monitoring. Drone technology is increasingly gaining traction among farmers because it offers new ways to boost crop yields through in-depth analysis, long-distance crop spraying, and high-efficiency crop analysis.

2. **Soil health monitoring and sowing of seeds:** With the use of sensors, cameras, and infrared rays that scan the soil for nutritional qualities, AI can be used to monitor soil health. This also aids in determining how individual seeds react to different soils, the impact of weather changes on the soil, and the likelihood of disease and insect dissemination.

3. **Irrigation and fertiliser management:** Real-time estimating can be done during the cultivation phase by producing a field map and identifying regions where crops require water, fertiliser, or pesticides using high-definition photographs from airborne devices (drones or copters). To a significant extent, this aids in resource optimization.

4. **Weed management:** Computer vision, robotics, and machine learning may all be used to successfully manage weeds. Data is collected using AI to check the weed infestation region, allowing farmers to spray chemicals only where the weeds are present. Pesticide and herbicide losses are reduced as a result of this method.

5. **Predicts advisories for pest attack:** A computer-aided system can effectively diagnose diseases and implement control measures. Pre-processing of a leaf picture segment into areas such as background, sick part, and non-diseased part. The sick area was then cropped and sent to distant labs for additional analysis. Image processing can also be used for pest identification and nutrient deficit detection.

6. **Precision Farming:** Precision farming is a type of farming that requires a high level of accuracy and control. High precision positioning system, geological mapping, remote sensing, integrated electronic communication, variable rate technology, optimum planting and harvesting time estimator, water resource management, plant and soil nutrient management, and pest and rodent attacks are some of the advanced technologies that enable precision farming. It entails applying farm inputs at the correct time, in the right place, and in the right amounts.

7. **Predict harvesting stages:** Images of several crops taken in a white/UV-free environment. The ripening stage of the crop/fruits is determined by capturing light. Depending on the crop/fruit category, farmers can identify different levels of readiness.

8. **Agricultural Product Monitoring and Storage Control:** In agriculture storage, drying, grading of harvested crops are also very important aspects. Monitoring and quality control mechanisms of agricultural products are employed by the concept of artificial intelligence.

9. **AI tools for accurate supply and demand information:** AI has made significant progress in agricultural demand and supply management. Its effective use in supply chain planning and optimization, including demand forecasting and logistics, can save farmers a lot of money and help stakeholders tackle the information asymmetry problem.

10. **Automation of Green House:** There are many factors that influence plant growth and the ripening of produce in green house. It is impossible for humans to analyse all these factors and know exactly how plants will grow. AI makes analysis of all these growth factors possible and provides highly accurate assessments of plant growth.

11. **Driverless Tractors:** Driverless tractors are self-contained tractors that conduct all farm tasks independently and precisely. They're outfitted with sensors that can carry out the necessary tasks, such as monitoring barriers and deciding where farm inputs should be applied. Agriculture is already merging off-the-shelf technologies like GPS systems, radars, and sensors to open up new farming opportunities.

12. **Weather Forecasting:** A variety of sensors, satellites and computer models are utilized by meteorologists to predict future weather patterns. Reinforcement learning is applied by artificial intelligence (AI) techniques considering past predictions and actual outcomes. Therefore, AI is efficiently working prediction to minimize the potential chances of crop losses and improve the productivity.

13. **Agricultural Drones:** Drones are being used in the agricultural sector to enhance many farming practices. The two types of drones- ground-based and aerial-based drones are being used in agriculture for crop health assessment, crop monitoring, spraying pesticides, irrigation, planting, and analysing the field. These drones capture multispectral, thermal, and visual imagery during their flight. The use of drones offers many benefits such as crop health imaging, integrated GIS mapping, saving time, ease of use, and also increasing crop yields. When we combine drone technology with proper strategy and planning based on real-time data collection, we can give a high-tech makeover to the agricultural sector.

Benefits of agri-drones

- Security: The drones are operated by trained drone pilots. So, there are no chances of their misuse.
- High efficiency: Drones do not have any operational delays and can work double the speed of human labor.
- Water-saving: In comparison to traditional spraying methods, agricultural drones use ultra-low volume (ULV) spraying technology, thus saving more water.
- Low cost and easy to maintain: Agri drones are sturdy, low in cost, and require minimum maintenance. Some of the key features include a detachable container, low-cost frame, precise spraying of pesticides.

Limitations of agri drones

- Connectivity issue: Often, online coverage is unavailable in rural areas. Under such circumstances, a farmer needs to invest in internet connectivity, which can turn into a recurring expense.
- Weather dependent: Drones do not have any operational delays and can work double the speed of human labor.
- Weather dependent: Drones are heavily dependent on good weather conditions. Under rainy or windy weather conditions, it is not advisable to fly drones.
- Knowledge and Skill: Using new technology is a welcoming change but using it daily requires the right skillset and adequate knowledge. An average farmer may struggle to understand drone functions. Either he must acquire the knowledge or remain dependent on an experienced person.

Open Challenges in Iot Based Agriculture

Various eminent researchers have worked hard towards the usage and impact of the Internet of Things (IoT) in agriculture. Many research challenges arise in IoT based Smart Agricultural applications. This research study has identified some unfolded IoT based smart agricultural challenges.

1. Protection of electronic circuits of devices used in IoT agricultural system from natural environmental situations (Heavy rain, fire, intolerable winds, extreme humidity, high/low temperature, etc.)
2. Reliable energy-efficient network-based setup for the secure transmission of information to respective stakeholders in a secured manner.

3. Selection of suitable IoT end devices, tools, and technologies for implementing smart farming.
4. Design and implementation of highly scalable and reliable security mechanism for each IoT end devices used in Smart Agriculture.
5. Resource utilization in an optimized manner is a big challenge in IoT agriculture.
6. Cost-analysis and mobility are also huge challenges for smart farming.
7. Maintenance of Quality of Service (QoS) efficiently in IoT based Smart Agricultural System is also an unfolded issue.
8. A proper decision-making system to handle the natural disaster with the latest policies is a part of these open challenges in IoT agriculture.
9. Crop residue for a clean environment is still a major problem.

Geographical Information Systems (GIS)

A Geographical Information System (GIS) is a system for capturing, storing, analyzing and managing data and associated attributes, which are spatially referenced to the Earth. GIS is a software tool that allows users to create interactive queries, analyze the spatial information, edit data, maps, and present the results of all these operations. GIS technology is becoming essential tool to combine various maps and remote sensing information to generate various models, which are used in real time environment.

Application of GIS

1. Geographical Information System (GIS) is the most important and useful system for decision making in Agricultural sector by the functionaries.
2. GIS will helps ascertain the ground level realities with the help of spatial data obtained from various resources.
3. In GIS one can integrate data from various sources such as Remote Sensing Data and Image with that of data of land records and agricultural census.
4. GIS applications can be used in agro-based enterprise to ascertain the scope of activities and monitoring of activities.

Remote Sensing Applications in Agriculture

The term "remote sensing" was coined by Ms Evelyn Pruitt in the mid-1950's. Remote Sensing (RS) is a technology that provides the means to collect and use geographic data to assist in the development of Agriculture. It is regarded as the most accepted meaning to instrument-based techniques employed in the acquisition and measurement of spatially organized or geographically distributed data on some properties such as spectral, spatial, physical of an array of target points of objects and materials from a distance from the observed target without physical contact. Remote sensing of the environment by geographers is usually done with the help of mechanical devices known as remote sensors. Remote sensing imagery has many applications in mapping land use and cover, agriculture, soils mapping, forestry, city planning, archaeological investigations, military observation, and geological surveying.

Applications of Remote Sensing and GIS Remote Sensing

It is an important tool to provide important information on soils, land evaluation, land degradation, crop distribution, crop growth, availability of water resources etc.

- Crop Production Databases
- Crop growth and yield determination
- Crop Monitoring
- Use of GIS in combination with remote sensing enhances the decision-making in the following ways:
- Process identification to enable comparison of different acquisitions through time.
- Identification of agricultural and other development problems.
- Evaluation of possible technical interventions for conservation or reclamation measures.
- Monitoring of soils, water, and land degradation processes.

Global Positioning System

The Global Positioning System (GPS) is a satellite-based radio-navigation system established by the U.S. Department of Defense for military positioning applications and as a by-product, has been made available to the civilian community. The successful application of GPS Technology has been seen in Navigation, surveying, and integration with Geographic Information Systems (GIS). It is also regarded as complex system which can be used to achieve positional accuracies ranging from 100 m to a few millimeters depending on the equipment used and procedures followed.

12

Data Collection and Management

Rishikesh Kumar

Agricultural Extension, School of Social Sciences, College of Post Graduate Studies in Agricultural Sciences, Umaim, CAU, Impal, Manipur

Data refers to any collection of facts, observations, measurements, or values that are typically numerical, but can also be qualitative. It's raw material that can be processed and organized to provide context, relevance, and meaning. In its raw form, data may not carry any specific meaning and might appear as a series of numbers, text, symbols, or images.

Types of Data

- Quantitative Data: Numerical data that can be measured and expressed with numbers (e.g., height, weight, temperature).
- Qualitative Data: Descriptive data that expresses qualities or characteristics, often observed and not easily quantified (e.g., colors, opinions, emotions).
- Categorical Data: Data that falls into specific categories or groups without a natural order (e.g., Types of fruits, gender, or education levels).
- Ordinal Data: Categorical data with a natural order or ranking (e.g., rankings, ratings).

Forms of Data

- Raw Data: The original data collected without any processing or manipulation.
- Processed Data: Raw data that has been organized, structured, or analyzed to make it more useful or understandable.

Importance of Data

- Decision Making: Data helps in making informed decisions by providing evidence and insights.

- Understanding Patterns: Analysis of data allows the identification of trends, patterns, and correlations.
- Improving Efficiency: Businesses and organizations use data to optimize processes and improve efficiency.
- Innovation: Data is crucial in driving innovation, research, and the development of new technologies.

Data Sources

- Sensors and Devices: Devices, sensors, and systems generate data in various forms, such as IoT devices, cameras, and wearables.
- Surveys and Studies: Data collected through surveys, questionnaires, and scientific studies.
- Digital Interactions: Online activities, social media interactions, and digital transactions generate vast amounts of data.

Challenges with Data

- Volume: The sheer volume of data generated can be overwhelming, leading to challenges in storage, processing, and analysis.
- Quality: Ensuring data accuracy, consistency, and reliability is essential for making sound decisions.
- Privacy and Security: Protecting sensitive data from unauthorized access or breaches is crucial.
- Interpretation: Making sense of data requires skills in analysis and interpretation to derive meaningful insights.

Data is a cornerstone in various fields, including business, science, technology, healthcare and driving progress and informing decisions when effectively collected, managed, and analyzed.

Data collection and management

Data collection and management involve the systematic gathering, organizing, storing, and processing of information to derive insights, make informed decisions, and solve problems. Here are steps and key considerations for effective data collection and management:

Data Collection

- Define Objectives: Clearly define the goals and objectives of the data collection process. Determine what specific information is needed and why.

- Choose Data Sources: Identify the sources from which data will be collected. Sources can include surveys, interviews, sensors, databases, or existing records.
- Select Data Collection Methods: Choose appropriate methods for gathering data, such as surveys, questionnaires, observations, or interviews. Consider the most suitable approach based on the nature of the information required.
- Design Data Collection Instruments: Develop tools, forms, or questionnaires to collect the required data. Ensure clarity, relevance, and accuracy in the questions or metrics used.
- Ethical Considerations: Adhere to ethical guidelines, ensuring that data collection respects privacy, confidentiality, and informed consent from participants.
- Collect Data: Execute the data collection process systematically, ensuring accuracy, completeness, and consistency in gathering information.

Data Management

- Data Organization and Storage: Organize collected data systematically, categorizing and storing it in a structured manner. Use databases, spreadsheets, or specialized software for efficient storage.
- Data Cleaning and Preprocessing: Review collected data to identify and rectify errors, inconsistencies, or missing information. Preprocess the data to ensure its quality and readiness for analysis.
- Data Security: Implement robust security measures to protect data from unauthorized access, breaches, or loss. Encryption, access controls, and regular backups are essential components.
- Data Integration: Combine data from various sources, if applicable, to create a unified dataset for comprehensive analysis.
- Data Analysis: Use analytical tools and techniques to derive insights, identify patterns, correlations, and trends within the collected data.
- Data Interpretation and Reporting: Interpret the analyzed data to draw meaningful conclusions and insights. Prepare reports, visualizations, or presentations to communicate findings effectively.
- Continuous Improvement: Regularly assess and refine data management processes to enhance efficiency, accuracy, and relevance.

Considerations for Effective Data Management

- Scalability: Ensure that data management systems can accommodate growing volumes of data without compromising efficiency.
- Data Governance: Establish clear protocols, policies, and responsibilities for managing data within an organization.
- Compliance: Adhere to legal and regulatory requirements concerning data privacy, protection, and usage.
- User Accessibility: Ensure authorized personnel have appropriate access to relevant data for decision-making purposes.

Effective data collection and management are crucial for organizations and individuals to harness the power of information, enabling better decision-making, improved operations, and innovation across various fields and industries.

System for data analytics

To establish a system for data analytics, you need to consider several key components and steps. Here's a high-level overview of the process:

3. **Define objectives**: Clearly define the objectives of your data analytics initiative. Determine the specific problems or questions you want to address through data analysis. This will help you stay focused and ensure that the system aligns with your goals.
4. **Data collection:** Identify the data sources relevant to your objectives. This may include internal data (e.g., databases, spreadsheets, transaction records) and external data (e.g., public datasets, third-party sources). Determine how you will collect, store, and organize the data. Consider data quality, security, and compliance requirements.
5. **Data integration and preprocessing:** Consolidate and integrate data from different sources into a unified format. Preprocess the data by cleaning, transforming, and filtering it to ensure consistency and remove any inconsistencies or errors. This step is crucial for ensuring data accuracy and usability in subsequent analysis.
6. **Data storage and infrastructure:** Establish an appropriate infrastructure to store and manage the data. This could involve using a data warehouse, a data lake, or a cloud-based storage solution. Consider the scalability, accessibility, and security requirements of your data storage system.

7. **Analytics tools and techniques:** Select the appropriate analytics tools and techniques based on your objectives and data characteristics. This may involve using statistical analysis, data mining, machine learning, or visualization tools. Choose tools that align with your team's skill set and the complexity of the analysis required.
8. **Data analysis and modeling:** Apply the selected analytics techniques to extract insights from the data. This could involve exploratory data analysis, hypothesis testing, predictive modeling, or other advanced analytics methods. Iteratively refine and validate your models to ensure accuracy and relevance.
9. **Interpretation and visualization:** Interpret the results of your analysis and present them in a meaningful and visually appealing way. Data visualization techniques, such as charts, graphs, and dashboards, can help communicate insights effectively to stakeholders and decision-makers.
10. **Decision-making and action:** Translate the insights gained from data analysis into actionable recommendations or decisions. Collaborate with stakeholders, such as management, domain experts, and end-users, to ensure the analysis results are understood and can be applied effectively.
11. **Monitoring and feedback:** Continuously monitor the performance of your data analytics system and gather feedback from users. Regularly assess the impact of your analytics initiatives and make improvements as needed. This iterative process allows for continuous learning and optimization.

Guidelines for Data analytics

- Define Objectives: Clearly outline goals and questions for analysis.
- Understand Data Quality: Assess data sources and ensure quality.
- Choose Tools Wisely: Select suitable analytics tools and techniques.
- Prepare and Clean Data: Cleanse and preprocess data for analysis.
- Explore and Visualize: Use visualizations to understand patterns.
- Conduct In-Depth Analysis: Apply statistical and predictive methods.
- Interpret and Communicate: Derive actionable insights and present findings clearly.
- Validate and Iterate: Verify results and refine analysis continually.

- Ensure Security and Compliance: Protect data and adhere to regulations.
- Foster Collaboration and Learning: Encourage teamwork and stay updated with advancements.

These guidelines help in effectively extracting insights, making informed decisions, and ensuring the accuracy and relevance of data analytics processes.

Big Data analytics for extension

Big Data analytics has become an integral part of many industries, including agriculture and extension services. The use of Big Data analytics in extension services can provide valuable insights and support decision-making processes for farmers, policymakers, and other stakeholders in the agriculture sector. Here are some ways Big Data analytics can be utilized in extension services:

Data-driven decision-making: Big Data analytics allows extension agents to analyze large volumes of data from various sources, such as weather data, soil data, crop yields, market prices, and historical trends. By applying advanced analytics techniques, such as predictive modeling and machine learning algorithms, extension agents can make data-driven decisions regarding crop selection, planting schedules, pest control measures, and resource allocation.

Precision agriculture: Big Data analytics can be used to optimize farming practices through precision agriculture techniques. By analyzing data collected from sensors, drones, satellites, and other sources, extension services can gain insights into crop health, soil conditions, irrigation needs, and nutrient management. This information enables farmers to apply inputs precisely where and when they are needed, reducing costs, minimizing environmental impact, and maximizing yields.

Early warning systems: Big Data analytics can help develop early warning systems for pests, diseases, and extreme weather events. By analyzing historical and real-time data, extension services can identify patterns and indicators of potential threats to crops. This allows farmers and extension agents to take proactive measures, such as implementing pest management strategies or adapting farming practices, to minimize losses and protect agricultural productivity.

Market analysis and price forecasting: Big Data analytics can be used to analyze market trends, consumer behavior, and pricing data. By integrating data from various sources, such as market reports, social media, and online platforms, extension services can provide farmers with valuable insights into market demand, price fluctuations, and consumer preferences. This information helps farmers make informed decisions about crop selection, production volumes, and marketing strategies.

Knowledge sharing and recommendations: Big Data analytics can support knowledge sharing and dissemination of best practices among farmers. By analyzing data collected from various sources, such as field trials, research studies, and farmer feedback, extension services can identify successful practices, generate recommendations, and deliver personalized advice to individual farmers. This enables the efficient transfer of knowledge and expertise, improving agricultural productivity and sustainability.

It's important to note that the successful implementation of Big Data analytics in extension services requires appropriate data collection, data management, and data privacy practices. Collaboration among stakeholders, including farmers, researchers, extension agents, and technology providers, is also crucial to ensure the effective use of Big Data analytics in agriculture extension.

Development of Agricultural simulations

The development of agriculture simulation involves creating computer models and simulations to simulate various aspects of agricultural systems. These simulations can help researchers, policymakers, and farmers gain insights into complex agricultural processes, evaluate different scenarios, and make informed decisions. Here are the key steps involved in developing an agriculture simulation:

1. **Identify objectives:** Determine the specific objectives of the agriculture simulation. Are you interested in studying crop growth, water management, pest control, or resource allocation? Clearly define the goals and scope of the simulation.

2. **Data collection and analysis:** Gather relevant data to support the simulation. This may include historical climate data, soil characteristics, crop physiology parameters, management practices, and other relevant information. Analyze the data to identify patterns, relationships, and trends that will be used as inputs in the simulation model.

3. **Model selection:** Choose an appropriate modeling approach for your simulation. There are various types of models used in agricultural simulations, including statistical models, mathematical models, and agent-based models. Select the model that best suits your objectives and available data.

4. **Model development:** Develop the simulation model based on the chosen modeling approach. This involves translating the agricultural processes

and relationships into mathematical equations or computer algorithms. Collaborate with domain experts and researchers in the field to ensure the model accurately represents the real-world system.

5. **Calibration and validation:** Calibrate the simulation model by adjusting model parameters to match observed data and known system behavior. Validate the model by comparing its outputs with independent data. This step ensures that the model accurately represents the real-world agricultural system.
6. **Scenario design and experimentation**: Define the scenarios and experiments you want to run with the simulation model. These scenarios may involve changes in climate conditions, management practices, input levels, or other relevant factors. Simulate different scenarios to understand the potential outcomes and evaluate the impacts of various interventions or strategies.
7. **Sensitivity analysis:** Perform sensitivity analysis to assess how changes in model parameters or inputs affect the simulation results. This analysis helps identify the most influential factors and their impact on the system. It also provides insights into the uncertainties and limitations of the simulation model.
8. **Visualization and interpretation:** Visualize the simulation results using graphs, charts, maps, or other visual representations. This makes it easier to understand and communicate the outcomes of the simulation. Interpret the results, identify patterns, and draw conclusions to inform decision-making and policy development.
9. **Iterative improvement:** Continuously refine and improve the simulation model based on feedback, new data, and advances in knowledge. Incorporate new research findings, technological advancements, and user feedback to enhance the accuracy and usefulness of the simulation.
10. **Collaboration and dissemination:** Collaborate with stakeholders, including researchers, policymakers, and farmers, to ensure the simulation meets their needs. Disseminate the simulation findings and insights through reports, presentations, workshops, and other channels to facilitate knowledge sharing and uptake.

Disruptive technologies Analysis

Disruptive technologies are innovations that significantly alter, replace, or create new markets, industries, or ways of doing things. They often challenge existing norms, practices, or products, leading to significant changes in various sectors. Analyzing disruptive technologies involves understanding their impact, adoption, and potential implications across industries. Here are key aspects to consider in their analysis:

1. **Internet of Things (IoT):** IoT enables the connection of physical devices and sensors to collect and exchange data. In agriculture, IoT can be used to monitor and manage various aspects such as soil moisture, weather conditions, crop health, and livestock. This data-driven approach allows farmers to make informed decisions, optimize resource allocation, and improve productivity.
2. **Artificial Intelligence (AI) and Machine Learning (ML): AI** and ML algorithms are being deployed in agriculture to analyze large amounts of data and make predictions or recommendations. These technologies can be used for crop disease detection, yield prediction, pest management, and precision agriculture. AI-powered systems can help farmers optimize resource usage, reduce waste, and increase efficiency.
3. **Robotics and Automation:** Robotics and automation technologies are being used to automate labor-intensive tasks in agriculture. Robotic systems can perform activities such as planting, harvesting, and sorting crops with precision and efficiency. Drones are also being used for aerial imaging, crop monitoring, and spraying pesticides. These technologies reduce human labor requirements and increase operational efficiency.
4. **Vertical Farming and Indoor Agriculture:** Vertical farming involves growing crops in vertically stacked layers or structures using controlled environments and artificial lighting. This approach maximizes land utilization, conserves water, and enables year-round production. Indoor agriculture utilizes hydroponics, aeroponics, or aquaponics systems to grow crops without soil. These technologies address land and climate limitations, reduce water usage, and provide localized food production.
5. **Blockchain:** Blockchain technology offers transparent and secure decentralized databases. In agriculture, blockchain can be used for traceability and supply chain management. It enables the tracking of food products from farm to table, ensuring transparency, authenticity, and quality control. Blockchain can help build trust among consumers, reduce fraud, and facilitate fair trade practices.
6. **Advanced Sensing Technologies:** Advanced sensing technologies, such as hyperspectral imaging and spectroscopy, can provide detailed

information about crops' health, nutrient content, and disease presence. These technologies allow farmers to identify and address issues at an early stage, optimize fertilization and irrigation, and improve overall crop quality.

7. **Gene Editing and Biotechnology:** Gene editing technologies like CRISPR-Cas9 are revolutionizing plant breeding and genetic modification. These technologies enable precise modifications in plant genomes, enhancing traits such as disease resistance, yield, and nutritional content. Biotechnology advancements also contribute to the development of drought-tolerant crops, pest-resistant varieties, and improved agricultural inputs.

These disruptive technologies have the potential to increase productivity, optimize resource utilization, and address various challenges faced by the agriculture industry, including food security, climate change, and sustainability. However, it is important to consider the ethical, regulatory, and socio-economic implications associated with the adoption of these technologies to ensure their responsible and equitable deployment.

13

Management of Information System

Afshan Jabeen

Department of Agricultural Extension Education, University of Agricultural Sciences, Raichur, Karnataka

Management of information system

A management information system (MIS) is an information system used for decision-making, coordination, control, analysis, and visualization of information in an organization. The study of management information systems involves people, processes and technology in an organizational context. MIS professionals help firms realize maximum benefit from investment in personnel, equipment and business processes. MIS is a people-oriented field with an emphasis on service through technology. MIS is a system that aids management in making, carrying out, and controlling decisions.

Importance of MIS

1) It helps in minimizing risk in decision-making
2) It processes the data and derives information out of them
3) It provides information about the various aspects of business
4) It helps the executives to avail the information regarding the functional areas quickly
5) It helps the HRD manager in finding out the requirements of the human resource, their wages and salary, performance appraisal, training, promotion, absenteeism and employee, turnover, which is useful in drafting sound HRD policies.

Characteristics of MIS

- Systems Approach: The information system adopts a comprehensive view, examining interconnected subsystems within an organization.
- Management Orientation: MIS development is management-driven, following a top-down approach that aligns with overall business

objectives. Continuous managerial involvement ensures policy adherence and system specification compliance.

- Needs-Based: MIS design caters to the information requirements of managers at different hierarchical levels.
- Exception Orientation: It's designed to report promptly on exceptional situations, ensuring immediate communication to decision-makers during abnormal circumstances.
- Future Focus: MIS doesn't solely provide historical data; it also furnishes future-oriented information based on projected actions.
- Integration: Integration is pivotal, enhancing the meaningfulness of information by offering a holistic view of interconnected subsystems.
- Common Data Flow: Emphasizes minimizing duplication, consolidating functions, and simplifying operations to streamline the flow of information, albeit with practical considerations.
- Long-Term Planning: MIS development spans extended periods, demanding substantial planning efforts.
- Sub-System Concept: While perceived as a unified entity, MIS is broken down into manageable, meaningful sub-systems.
- Centralized Database: An integral feature involves a unified database encompassing the entire MIS structure.

Functions of MIS

1. **Data Capture:** MIS acquires data from internal and external sources within an organization, utilizing manual input or computer terminals. End users either record transactions on physical mediums like paper forms or directly input data into the computer system.
2. **Data Processing:** Captured data undergoes processing to transform it into necessary management information. Processing involves activities such as calculation, comparison, sorting, classification, and summarization. These actions organize, analyze, and manipulate data using statistical, mathematical, or operational models.
3. **Information Storage:** MIS stores processed or raw data for future utilization. Information not immediately required is preserved as organizational records. This activity organizes and retains data in an orderly manner for potential future use, often arranged into fields, records, files, or databases.

4. **Information Retrieval:** MIS retrieves stored information as per the needs of various users within the organization. The retrieved information is provided either directly to fulfill management information demands or undergoes further processing to meet specific requirements.
5. **Information Dissemination:** The refined information generated by MIS is disseminated to organizational users. Dissemination can occur periodically through reports or instantly via online access through computer terminals.

Role of MIS in an Organization

The role of the MIS in an organization can be compared to the role of the heart in the body. The information is the blood and MIS is the heart. In the body, the heart plays the role of supplying pure blood to all the elements of the body including the brain. The heart works faster and supplies more blood when needed. It regulates and controls the incoming impure blood, processes it and sends it to the destination in the quantity needed. It fulfils the needs of blood supply to the human body in the normal course and also in crisis. The MIS plays exactly the same role in the organization.

1. The system ensures that an appropriate data is collected from the various sources, processed, and sent further to all the needy destinations. The system is expected to fulfill the information needs of an individual, a group of individuals, the management functionaries: the managers and the top management.
2. The MIS satisfies the diverse needs through a variety of systems such as Query Systems, Analysis Systems, Modeling Systems and Decision Support Systems the MIS helps in Strategic Planning, Management Control, Operational Control and Transaction Processing.
3. The MIS helps the clerical personnel in the transaction processing and answers their queries on the data pertaining to the transaction, the status of a particular record and references on a variety of documents. The MIS helps the junior management personnel by providing the operational data for planning, scheduling and control, and helps them further in decision making at the operations level to correct an out-of-control situation.
4. The MIS helps the middle management in short them planning, target setting and controlling the business functions. It is supported by the use of the management tools of planning and control. The MIS helps the top management in goal setting, strategic planning and evolving the business plans and their implementation.

5. The MIS plays the role of information generation, communication, problem identification and helps in the process of decision making. The MIS, therefore, plays a vital role in the management, administration and operations of an organization.

14

Computer Networking

Wangshitula Longchar

Agricultural Extension, School of Social Sciences, College of Post Graduate Studies in Agricultural Sciences, Umaim, CAU, Impal, Manipur

In the broadest sense, a network is any interconnected group of people or things capable of sharing meaningful information with one another. In a technology context, the network is usually short for "computer network" or "data network" and implies that computers are the things sharing meaningful information. At a conceptual level, all data networks consist of nodes, which refers to any computer or digital device using the network and links, the physical connections (either wired or wireless) that carry messages between nodes.

Basic Networking Concept

Client/Server

Client/server describes the relationship between two computer programs in which one program, the client, makes a service request from another program, the server, which fulfils the request. Although the client/server idea can be used by programs within a single computer, it is a more important idea in a network. In a network, the client/server model provides a convenient way to interconnect programs that are distributed efficiently across different locations. Computer transactions using the client/server model are very common.

Hub

This is a hardware device that is used to network multiple computers together. It is a central connection for all the computers in a network, which is usually Ethernet-based. Information sent to the hub can flow to any other computer on the network. If you need to connect more than two computers together, a hub will allow you to do so. If you only need to network two computers together, a simple crossover Ethernet cable will do the trick.

Switch

A switch is used to network multiple computers together. Switches made for the consumer market are typically small, flat boxes with 4 to 8 Ethernet ports. These ports can connect to computers, cable or DSL modems, and other switches. High-end switches can have more than 50 ports and often are rack mounted. Switches are more advanced than hubs and less capable than routers. Unlike hubs, switches can limit the traffic to and from each port so that each device connected to the switch has a sufficient amount of bandwidth. For this reason, you can think of a switch as a "smart hub." However, switches don't provide the firewall and logging capabilities that routers do. Routers can often be configured by software (typically via a Web interface), while switches only work the way the hardware was designed.

Router

A hardware device designed to take incoming packets, analyze the packets and then direct them to the appropriate locations, moving the packets to another network, converting the packets to be moved across a different network interface, dropping the packets, or performing any other number of other actions. It can analyze the data being sent over a network, change how it is packaged and send it to another network or over a different network.

Network Topology

Network Topology refers to the physical or logical arrangement of devices and connections in a computer network, defining its structure and layout.

Bus

In a bus network, each computer is connected to a single communication cable via an interface and every computer can directly communicate with each other. The bus is a single pair or a bunch of wires that carry the electrical signals. The individual nodes are connected to the bus using a passive tap such that all systems are able to monitor the signal on the bus simultaneously. The bus acts as a broadcast medium. Access and control of bus network are typically maintained by a method called contention whereby if a line is unused a terminal or device can transmit its message at will but if two or more terminal initiate message simultaneously, they must stop and transmit again at different intervals. Traffic travels in both directions.

Advantages

- Easy to connect a computer or peripheral to a linear bus.
- Requires less cable length than a star topology.

Disadvantages

- Entire network shuts down if there is a break in the main cable.
- Terminators are required at both ends of the backbone cable.
- Difficult to identify the problem if the entire network shuts down.
- Not meant to be used as a stand-alone solution in a large building.

Star

A star topology is designed with each node (file server, workstations, and peripherals) connected directly to a central network hub, switch, or concentrator. Data on a star network passes through the hub, switch, or concentrator before continuing to its destination. The hub, switch, or concentrator manages and controls all functions of the network. It also acts as a repeater for the data flow. This configuration is common with twisted pair cable; however, it can also be used with coaxial cable or fibre optic cable.

Advantages

- Easy to install and wire.
- No disruptions to the network when connecting or removing devices.
- Computer Networking
- Easy to detect faults and to remove parts.

Disadvantages

- Requires more cable length than a linear topology.
- If the hub, switch, or concentrator fails, nodes attached are disabled.
- More expensive than linear bus topologies because of the cost of the hubs, etc.

Ring

In a ring network, every device has exactly two neighbours for communication purposes. All messages travel through a ring in the same direction (either "clockwise" or "counter clockwise"). A failure in any cable or device breaks the loop and can take down the entire network. To implement this network, one typically uses FDDI, SONET, or Token Ring technology. These topologies are found in some office buildings or school campuses.

Advantages

- This type of network topology is very organized. Each node gets to send the data when it receives an empty token. This helps to reduces chances of collision. Also, in ring topology all the traffic flows in only one direction at very high speed.
- Even when the load on the network increases, its performance is better than that of Bus topology.
- There is no need for network server to control the connectivity between workstations.
- Additional components do not affect the performance of network.
- Each computer has equal access to resources.

Disadvantages

- Each packet of data must pass through all the computers between source and destination. This makes it slower than Star topology.
- If one workstation or port goes down, the entire network gets affected.
- Network is highly dependent on the wire which connects different components.
- MAU's and network cards are expensive as compared to Ethernet cards and hubs.

Tree

A tree topology combines characteristics of linear bus and star topologies. It consists of groups of star-configured workstations connected to a linear bus backbone cable. Tree topologies allow for the expansion of an existing network, and enable schools to configure a network to meet their needs.

Advantages

- Point-to-point wiring for individual segments.
- Supported by several hardware and software vendors.

Disadvantages

- Overall length of each segment is limited by the type of cabling used.
- If the backbone line breaks, the entire segment goes down.
- More difficult to configure and wire than other topologies.

Mesh

Mesh topologies involve the concept of routes. Unlike each of the previous topologies, messages sent on a mesh network can take any of several possible paths from source to destination. (Recall that even in a ring, although two cable paths exist, messages can only travel in one direction.) Some WANs, most notably the Internet, employ mesh routing. A mesh network in which every device connects to every other is called a full mesh.

Advantages

- Data can be transmitted from different devices simultaneously. This topology can
- Withstand high traffic.
- Even if one of the components fails there is always an alternative present. So data transfer doesn't get affected.
- Expansion and modification in topology can be done without disrupting other nodes.

Disadvantages

- There are high chances of redundancy in many of the network connections.
- Overall cost of this network is way too high as compared to other network topologies.
- Set-up and maintenance of this topology is very difficult. Even administration of the network is tough.

Types of Networks: Depending upon the geographical area covered by a network, it is classified as:

1. Local Area Network (LAN)
2. Metropolitan Area Network (MAN)
3. Wide Area Network (WAN)
4. Personal Area Network (PAN)

Local Area Network (LAN)

LAN is a network that is used for communicating among computer devices, usually within an office building or home. It enables the sharing of resources such as files or hardware devices that may be needed by multiple users. It is limited in size, typically spanning a few hundred meters and no more than a mile. It is fast, with speeds from 10 Mbps to 10 Gbps and requires little wiring, typically a single cable connecting to each device. It has lower cost compared to MAN's or WAN's. It can be either wired or wireless. Twisted pair, coax or fibre optic cable can be used in wired LAN's. Every LAN uses a protocol – a set of rules that governs how packets are configured and transmitted. Nodes in a LAN are linked together with a certain topology. These topologies include: Bus, Ring and Star. They are capable of very high transmission rates (100s Mb/s to Gb/s).

Metropolitan Area Network (MAN)

A metropolitan area network (MAN) is a large computer network that usually spans a city or a large campus. It is optimized for a larger geographical area than a LAN, ranging from several blocks of buildings to entire cities. It might be owned and operated by a single organization, but it usually will be used by many individuals and organizations. It often acts as a high speed network to allow sharing of regional resources. It typically covers an area of between 5 and 50 km diameter. **Examples** - Telephone company network that provides a high speed DSL to customers and cable TV network.

Wide Area Network (WAN)

It covers a large geographic area such as country, continent or even whole of the world. It is two or more LANs connected together. The LANs can be many miles apart. To cover great distances, WANs may transmit data over leased high-speed phone lines or wireless links such as satellites. Multiple LANs can be connected together using devices such as bridges, routers, or gateways, which enable them to share data. The world's most popular WAN is the Internet.

Personal Area Network (PAN)

It is a network that is used for communicating among computers and computer devices (including telephones) in close proximity of around a few meters within a room. It can be used for communicating between the devices themselves, or for connecting to a larger network such as the internet. It can be wired or wireless. It is a computer network used for communication among computer devices, including telephones and personal digital assistants, in proximity to an individual's body. The devices may or may not belong to the person in question. The reach of a PAN is typically a few meters.

Wireless Sensor Networks in Agriculture

Agriculture and its related sectors are major source of income for people of India. Varying land and climate conditions prevailing in the country provides new challenges and opportunities in this sector. Wireless Sensor Networks (WSN) is a promising technology to address some of issues like soil management, pest management, water management, yield estimation, precision agriculture and macro and micro – climate monitoring. WSN consists of tiny devices called motes capable of sensing the environment surrounding them, processing the data and communicating the sensed information in a collaborative, self-organizing and power-efficient manner. The system architecture of a WSN deployment consists of group of motes sensing the environment in which they have been deployed and communicating the sensed data to a central location from where the data can be stored or further processes paving the way for new and interesting applications in Agriculture. The sensors that can be interfaced with these motes reveal the various micro and micro-climatic conditions prevailing in the field of deployment. The sensors that are useful for agriculture include Temperature (T), Relative Humidity (RH), Soil Moisture (SM), Soil temperature (ST), leaf Wetness (LW), Rain gauze (Rg), Solar Radiation (SR), Wind speed and Wind direction (WSD), Soil conductivity (EC) AND Ph. The weather information acquired for examples used in pest prediction, calculation of Evapotranspiration (ET), soil profiling, water management and over fertilization.

Open Technology Computing Facilities

Open technology computing facilities refer to computing facilities that embrace open-source technologies and principles. These facilities are built on open standards, open hardware, and open software, allowing users to have greater control, transparency, and collaboration in the computing environment.

Here are a few key aspects of open technology computing facilities:

1. **Open Standards:** Open technology computing facilities adhere to open standards, which are publicly available specifications for hardware or software interfaces. Open standards ensure interoperability and allow different systems to work together seamlessly. Examples of open standards include HTML, HTTP, and JSON.

2. **Open Hardware:** Open technology computing facilities may utilize open hardware designs. Open hardware refers to hardware components whose specifications are publicly available, allowing users to study, modify, and distribute them. Open hardware fosters innovation and enables users to customize and adapt hardware to their specific needs.

3. **Open Software:** Open technology computing facilities primarily rely on open-source software. Open-source software is distributed with its source code, allowing users to view, modify, and distribute it freely. This fosters collaboration, innovation, and community-driven development. Examples of open-source software include the Linux operating system, Apache web server, and MySQL database.

4. **Community-driven Development**: Open technology computing facilities often encourage community participation and collaboration. Developers, users, and enthusiasts can contribute to the development and improvement of the software and hardware components. This collective effort leads to faster innovation, bug fixes, and feature enhancements.

5. **Transparency and Security:** Open technology computing facilities prioritize transparency, allowing users to inspect the source code and verify its security and integrity. The open nature of the technology facilitates the identification and resolution of vulnerabilities, promoting overall system security.

6. **Flexibility and Customizability:** Open technology computing facilities provide users with the flexibility to tailor the software and hardware components according to their requirements. Users can modify the source code, add new features, or integrate with other systems, enabling customization and adaptability.

Open technology computing facilities are widely used in various domains, including cloud computing, data centers, scientific research, and education. They promote openness, collaboration, and innovation, empowering users to have more control over their computing infrastructure.

15

Human-Computer Interaction (HCI)

Soujanya Kotte

College of Agriculture, Rajendranagar
Professor Jayashankar Telangana State Agricultural University, Hyderabad

HCI is the study of how people interact with computers, especially as it relates to technology design. User-centered design, UI and UX are combined with HCI to provide intuitive technology and products.

Human-computer interaction (HCI) is the field of study that focuses on optimizing how users and computers interact by designing interactive computer interfaces that satisfy users' needs. It is a multidisciplinary subject covering computer science, behavioral sciences, cognitive science, ergonomics, psychology, and design principles. HCI focuses on designing, implementing and evaluating interactive interfaces that enhance user experience using computing devices. This includes user interface design, user-centered design, and user experience design.

The Rise of HCI

- HCI emerged in the early 1980s. In a short period of time, the research area expanded to practically encompass all IT.
- It changed everything when Apple introduced the Macintosh in 1984. The usage of computers has become much more accessible, making communication simpler. Keyboard, mouse, and icon-based user interfaces were popular during this period.
- With the advent of the internet and the explosion of mobile and diversified technologies such as voice-based and Internet of Things (IoT), computing became omnipresent and omnipotent. Technological competence further led to the evolution of user interactions. Consequently, the need for developing a tool that would make such man-machine interactions more human-like grew significantly. This established HCI as a technology, bringing different fields such as cognitive engineering, linguistics, neuroscience and others under its realm.

Importance of HCI

- The study of human-computer interaction aims to create a conversation between people and machines that seems natural and intuitive.
- A superior user experience that doesn't necessitate a lot of physical or mental effort is what designers and product developers strive to achieve.
- Humans use digital devices to do various jobs, and effective human-computer
- interfaces are essential. Lack of consideration for human-computer interaction can result in poorly designed user interfaces that have an adverse effect on product usability and raise the likelihood of product failure.
- Designers can gain invaluable knowledge about ergonomics, usability, user behaviors, emotional responses, user goals, and user personas by researching human-computer interaction.
- The ultimate goal of HCI is to reduce the amount of effort a user expends when using technology. It aspires to make interactions between people and computers as simple, natural, and open-ended as interactions between people.

Key components of HCI: Fundamentally, HCI is made up of four key components:

1. **The user:** The user component refers to an individual or a group of individuals that participate in a common task. HCI studies users' needs, goals, and interaction patterns. It analyzes various parameters such as users' cognitive capabilities, emotions, and experiences to provide them with a seamless experience while interacting with computing systems.
2. **The goal-oriented task:** A user operates a computer system with an objective or goal in mind. The computer provides a digital representation of objects to accomplish this goal. For example, booking an airline for a destination could be a task for an aviation website. In such goal-oriented scenarios, one should consider the following aspects for a better user experience:
    - The complexity of the task that the user intends to accomplish
    - Knowledge and skills necessary to interact with the digital object
    - Time required to carry out the task

3. **The interface:** The interface is a crucial HCI component that can enhance the overall user interaction experience. Various interface-related aspects must be considered, such as interaction type (touch, click, gesture, or voice), screen resolution, display size, or even color contrast. Users can adjust these depending on the user's needs and requirements.
4. **The context:** HCI is not only about providing better communication between users and computers but also about factoring in the context and environment in which the system is accessed. For example, while designing a smartphone app, designers need to evaluate how the app will visually appear in different lighting conditions (during day or night) or how it will perform when there is a poor network connection. Such aspects can have a significant impact on the end-user experience.

Examples of HCI

1. IoT technology

IoT devices and applications have significantly impacted our daily lives. According to a May 2022 report by IoT Analytics, global IoT endpoints are expected to reach 14.4 billion in 2022 and grow to 27 billion (approx.) by 2025. As users interact with such devices, they tend to collect their data, which helps understand different user interaction patterns. IoT companies can make critical business decisions that can eventually drive their future revenues and profits.

2. Eye-tracking Technology

Eye-tracking is about detecting where a person is looking based on the gaze point. Eye-tracking devices use cameras to capture the user's gaze along with some embedded light sources for clarity. Moreover, these devices use machine learning algorithms and image processing capabilities for accurate gaze detection. Other applications include 'driver monitoring systems' that ensure road security. Moreover, in the future, HCI-enabled eye-tracking systems may allow users to scroll through a computer screen just by rolling their eyeballs.

3. Speech Recognition Technology

Speech recognition technology interprets human language, derives meaning from it, and performs the task for the user. Recently, this technology has gained significant popularity with the emergence of chatbots and virtual assistants.

For example, products such as Amazon's Alexa, Microsoft's Cortana, Google's Google Assistant, and Apple's Siri employ speech recognition to enable user interaction with their devices, cars, etc. The combination of HCI and speech recognition further fine-tune man-machine interactions that allow the devices to interpret and respond to users' commands and questions with maximum accuracy. It has various applications, such as transcribing conference calls, training sessions, and interviews.

4. AR/VR Technology

AR and VR are immersive technologies that allow humans to interact with the digital world and increase the productivity of their daily tasks. For example, smart glasses enable hands-free and seamless user interaction with computing systems. Consider an example of a chef who intends to learn a new recipe. With smart glass technology, the chef can learn and prepare the target dish simultaneously.

Moreover, the technology also reduces system downtime significantly. This implies that as smart AR/VR glasses such as 'Oculus Quest 2' are supported by apps, the faults or problems in the system can be resolved by maintenance teams in real-time. This enhances user experience in a minimum time span. Also, the glasses can detect the user's response to the interface and further optimize the interaction based on the user's personality, needs, and preferences.

5. Cloud Computing

Today, companies across different fields are embracing remote task forces. According to a 'Breaking Barriers 2020' survey by Fuze (An 8×8 Company), around 83% of employees feel more productive working remotely. Considering the current trend, conventional workplaces will witness a massive rejig and transform entirely in a couple of decades. Thanks to cloud computing and human-computer interaction, such flexible offices have become a reality.

Moreover, an employee can access data on the cloud from any physical location by exploiting cloud-based SaaS services. Such virtual settings streamline workflows and support seamless collaboration with remote teams across industry verticals without impacting productivity. Thus, with time, the idea of traditional offices will cease to exist, mainly because of SaaS and HCI.

Goals of HCI

The principal objective of HCI is to develop functional systems that are usable, safe, and efficient for end-users. The developer community can achieve this goal by fulfilling the following criteria:

- Have sound knowledge of how users use computing systems
- Design methods, techniques, and tools that allow users to access systems based on their needs.

- Adjust, test, refine, validate, and ensure that users achieve effective communication or interaction with the systems.
- Always give priority to end-users and lay the robust foundation of HCI
- To realize the above points, developers must focus on two relevant areas: usability and user experience

Usability

Usability is key to HCI as it ensures that users of all types can quickly learn and use computing systems. A practical and usable HCI system has the following characteristics:

How to use it: This should be easy to learn and remember for new and infrequent users to learn and remember. For example, operating systems with a user-friendly interface are easier to understand than DOS operating systems that use a command-line interface.

- Safe: A safe system safeguards users from undesirable and dangerous situations. This may refer to users making mistakes and errors while using the system that may lead to severe consequences. Users can resolve this through HCI practices. For example, systems can be designed to prevent users from activating specific keys or buttons accidentally. Another example could be to provide recovery plans once the user commits mistakes. This may give users the confidence to explore the system or interface further.
- Efficient: An efficient system defines how good the system is and whether it accomplishes the tasks that it is supposed to. Moreover, it illustrates how the system provides the necessary support to users to complete their tasks.
- Effective: A practical system provides high-quality performance. It describes whether the system can achieve the desired goals.
- Utility: Utility refers to the various functionalities and tools provided by the system to complete the intended task. For example, a sound utility system offers an integrated development environment (IDE) that provides intermittent help to programmers or users through suggestions.
- Enjoyable: Users find the computing system enjoyable to use when the interface is less complex to interpret and understand.

2. User experience

User experience is a subjective trait that focuses on how users feel about the computing system when interacting with it. Here, user feelings are studied individually so that developers and support teams can target particular users to evoke positive feelings while using the system. HCI systems classify user interaction patterns into the following categories and further refine the system based on the detected pattern:

- **Desirable traits** – satisfying, enjoyable, motivating, or surprising
- **Undesirable traits** – Frustrating, unpleasant, or annoying

Designing ICT gadgets based on human interaction principles

It involves considering how people interact with technology and creating devices that are intuitive, user-friendly, and accessible. Here are some key principles to consider when designing ICT gadgets based on human interaction:

- **User-Centered Design**: Put the needs and preferences of the end-users at the centre of the design process. Understand their goals, tasks, and challenges to create devices that align with their requirements and expectations.
- **Simplicity and Ease of Use:** Strive for simplicity in design, making the gadgets easy to understand and use. Minimize complexity, eliminate unnecessary steps, and provide clear instructions and feedback to users.
- **Consistency and Familiarity:** Follow established design conventions and patterns to ensure consistency across different gadgets and applications. Use familiar icons, symbols, and interactions that users are already familiar with to reduce the learning curve.
- **Responsive and Intuitive Interfaces**: Design interfaces that respond quickly and smoothly to user inputs. Use visual cues, animations, and feedback to provide clear indications of actions and system responses.
- **Accessibility and Inclusivity:** Consider the diverse needs of users, including those with disabilities or limitations. Design gadgets that are accessible and usable by people with varying abilities, providing options for customization and alternative interaction methods.
- **Contextual Awareness:** Make gadgets contextually aware by leveraging sensors and data to adapt to the user's environment. For example, adjusting screen brightness based on ambient light or providing location-based suggestions.

- **Error Prevention and Recovery:** Anticipate potential user errors and design gadgets to prevent or minimize the impact of mistakes. Provide clear error messages, undo/redo functionality, and easy recovery options to enhance user confidence.
- **User Feedback and Iterative Design:** Seek feedback from users throughout the design process and iterate on the design based on their input. Conduct usability tests and observe how users interact with the gadgets to identify areas for improvement.
- **Scalability and Future-Proofing:** Design gadgets with scalability in mind, allowing for future updates and enhancements. Consider technological advancements and evolving user needs to ensure the longevity of the gadgets.
- **Ethical Considerations:** Consider ethical implications such as data privacy, security, and responsible use of technology. Design gadgets that respect user privacy and empower users to control their data.

By applying these principles, ICT gadgets can be designed to enhance user experience, promote usability, and ensure that technology adapts to human needs and behaviors.

Designing ICT gadgets based on interactive design

Interactive Design refers to the process of creating digital products, interfaces, or experiences that encourage active user engagement and participation. It involves designing interfaces and interactions that allow users to interact with the content, manipulate elements, and control the overall experience.

The importance of interactive design lies in its ability to enhance user engagement and provide a more personalized and immersive experience. Here are a few key reasons why interactive design is significant:

User Engagement: Interactive design facilitates meaningful interactions between users and digital products or interfaces. By providing interactive elements such as clickable buttons, draggable elements, or animations, it encourages users to actively engage with the content. This engagement can lead to increased user satisfaction, longer periods of interaction, and a higher likelihood of achieving the intended goals.

User-Centered Approach: Interactive design puts the user at the centre of the design process. It focuses on understanding user needs, preferences, and behaviors to create interfaces that are intuitive, easy to use, and enjoyable. By incorporating interactive elements, designers can design experiences that align with users' mental models, allowing them to navigate and interact with the interface in a natural and intuitive manner.

Enhanced Communication: Interactive design enables effective communication between users and digital products. It allows users to interact with elements, provide input, and receive feedback, fostering a sense of control and responsiveness. Through interactive elements, designers can convey information, guide users, and facilitate clear communication, resulting in a more efficient and engaging user experience.

Personalization and Customization: Interactive design empowers users to personalize their experiences based on their preferences and needs. By incorporating interactive features like customizable settings, adaptive interfaces, or interactive dashboards, designers can provide users with the ability to tailor the experience to their liking. This customization enhances user satisfaction and creates a sense of ownership over the digital product or interface.

Emotional Connection: Interactive design has the potential to evoke emotional responses from users. Through interactive elements, designers can create experiences that trigger positive emotions, such as delight, surprise, or satisfaction. By designing interactive interfaces that are visually appealing, aesthetically pleasing, and provide feedback, designers can establish a stronger emotional connection between users and the product or interface.

Iterative Improvement: Interactive design allows for continuous improvement through iterative design processes. By observing user interactions, gathering feedback, and analyzing data, designers can identify areas of improvement and refine the interactive elements accordingly. This iterative approach ensures that the design remains relevant, effective, and aligned with user expectations.

Overall, interactive design plays a crucial role in creating engaging, user-centric, and memorable digital experiences. By focusing on user engagement, personalization, and effective communication, designers can create interfaces and products that not only meet user needs but also leave a lasting impact.

Approaches of Interactive Design

Interactive design encompasses various approaches and principles that aim to create engaging and user-centred digital experiences. Here are some common approaches used in interactive design:

User-Centered Design (UCD)

It is an approach that places the needs, goals, and preferences of users at the forefront of the design process. It involves understanding the target users, their context of use, and their requirements to create products or services that meet their expectations and deliver a satisfying user experience. Here are the key principles and steps involved in user-centered design:

- **User Research:** User research involves gathering data about the target users through various methods such as interviews, surveys, observations, and usability testing. It aims to gain insights into their behaviors, needs, motivations, and pain points. The data collected helps designers understand the users and their context, which informs the subsequent design decisions.
- **User Personas**: Personas are fictional representations of the target users based on research data. They embody typical user characteristics, goals, and behaviors, and serve as a reference for design decisions. Personas humanize the user and help designers empathize with their needs, enabling them to create user-centric solutions.
- **Task Analysis:** Task analysis involves breaking down user activities and goals into smaller, manageable tasks. It helps designers understand the steps users take to achieve their objectives and identify pain points, inefficiencies, or opportunities for improvement. Task analysis informs the design of intuitive and efficient workflows.
- **Information Architecture:** Information architecture (IA) is the process of organizing and structuring information within a digital product. It involves creating clear hierarchies, defining navigation systems, and labeling content to help users find what they need quickly and easily. IA ensures that the product's information is organized in a logical and user-friendly manner.
- **Prototyping and Iterative Design:** Prototyping involves creating low-fidelity or high-fidelity representations of the product to test and gather feedback from users. Through iterations, designers refine the design based on user feedback and insights. This iterative process allows for continuous improvement and ensures that the design aligns with user needs.
- **Usability Testing:** Usability testing involves observing users as they interact with the product or prototype and collecting feedback on its usability and user experience. By watching users perform tasks and listening to their feedback, designers can identify usability issues, pain points, and areas of improvement. Usability testing helps validate design decisions and ensures that the final product meets user expectations.

- **Accessibility Considerations:** User-centered design also includes considering the needs of users with disabilities and ensuring that the product is accessible to a diverse range of users. Designers should follow accessibility guidelines and best practices to ensure that the product is inclusive and usable for everyone.

By embracing user-centered design principles and practices, designers can create products that are intuitive, enjoyable, and useful to the target users. It helps reduce the risk of developing products that do not meet user needs and increases the chances of creating successful and impactful user experiences.

Activity Centered Design

Activity-centered design is a user-centered design approach that focuses on understanding and designing for the specific activities or tasks that users perform. It aims to create products, services, or systems that effectively support and enhance these activities. In activity-centered design, the emphasis is placed on the context of use and the goals and needs of the users. Designers strive to gain a deep understanding of the activities that users engage in, the goals they want to achieve, and the challenges they face during these activities. This understanding helps guide the design process and ensures that the resulting product or system aligns with users' needs and expectations.

The key steps in activity-centered design typically include:

- **Activity Analysis:** This involves studying and analyzing the activities performed by users, including their goals, workflow, and context. It may involve user observations, interviews, and surveys to gather data.
- **Task Modeling**: Task modeling involves breaking down the activities into smaller tasks or subtasks, identifying the sequence of steps, and understanding the dependencies and relationships between them. This helps designers identify potential areas for improvement or optimization.
- **Conceptual Design**: In this phase, designers generate ideas and concepts for the design solution. They explore various possibilities to address user needs and enhance the activities identified earlier. Sketching, prototyping, and brainstorming are common techniques used in this phase.
- **Iterative Design:** The design is developed and refined through iterations, incorporating user feedback and evaluation. Prototypes or mock-ups are often created to gather feedback early in the process and make necessary adjustments based on user insights.

- **Evaluation and Testing:** The designed solution is evaluated with users to assess its effectiveness, usability, and alignment with their activities and goals. This can involve usability testing, user feedback sessions, and other evaluation methods to validate and refine the design.
- **Implementation:** Once the design is finalized, it is implemented and developed into a functional product, service, or system. This may involve collaboration with developers, engineers, and other stakeholders to ensure the design intent is properly realized.

System Design Approach

The system design approach for interactive design involves a systematic process of designing and developing interactive systems or applications that provide engaging and meaningful user experiences. This approach typically includes the following steps:

- **User Research:** Understand the target audience, their needs, preferences, and behaviors through methods like interviews, surveys, and observations. Identify user goals and tasks to be supported by the interactive system.
- **Conceptual Design**: Define the overall concept and scope of the interactive system. Create user personas, scenarios, and user flows to capture the intended user interactions and workflows.
- **Information Architecture:** Organize and structure the content and functionality of the interactive system. Develop navigation systems, sitemaps, and wireframes to represent the overall structure and hierarchy of the system.
- **Interaction Design:** Design the interactive elements and user interface components that enable users to interact with the system. Consider usability principles and best practices to create intuitive and efficient user interfaces. Use techniques like storyboarding, prototyping, and mockups to visualize the interactions.
- **Visual Design:** Apply visual aesthetics to the user interface, including color schemes, typography, imagery, and branding elements. Ensure visual consistency and alignment with the overall concept and target audience preferences.
- **Prototyping and Testing**: Create interactive prototypes to simulate user interactions and test the design assumptions. Conduct usability testing and gather feedback to identify areas of improvement and refine the design.

- **Development and Implementation:** Translate the design into actual software code or implementation. Collaborate with developers and engineers to ensure the design is accurately implemented and functions as intended.
- **Iterative Design:** Continuously evaluate and refine the interactive design based on user feedback and real-world usage.Use analytics and user testing to identify areas for improvement and make iterative design changes.
- **User Documentation and Training:** Create user guides, tutorials, and help documentation to assist users in understanding and effectively using the interactive system. Provide training resources if necessary.
- **Maintenance and Updates:** Regularly maintain and update the interactive system to address bugs, security vulnerabilities, and incorporate new features or enhancements based on user feedback and changing requirements.

Genius Design Approach

The genius design approach to interactive design involves creating user experiences that are intuitive, engaging, and memorable. It focuses on understanding the needs, behaviors, and preferences of the users to design interactions that are both functional and enjoyable. Here are some key principles and strategies that can contribute to a genius design approach in interactive design:

- **User-Centered Design**: Put the user at the center of the design process. Understand their goals, motivations, and challenges. Conduct user research, interviews, and usability testing to gather insights and validate design decisions.
- **Simplicity:** Strive for simplicity and minimalism in design. Eliminate unnecessary elements and streamline interactions. Use clear and concise language, intuitive navigation, and visual hierarchy to guide users through the experience.
- **Consistency:** Maintain consistency in design elements, such as colors, typography, and layouts, to create a cohesive and familiar user interface. Consistent interactions and behavior patterns enhance learnability and make the experience more intuitive.
- **Feedback and Responsiveness:** Provide immediate and meaningful feedback to users when they perform actions. Visual cues, animations,

and progress indicators help users understand the system's response and build trust in the interaction.

- **Contextual Awareness:** Design interactions that adapt to the user's context and environment. Consider factors like device capabilities, screen sizes, input methods, and user locations to create responsive and personalized experiences.
- **Delightful Interactions:** Surprise and delight users through creative and engaging interactions. Incorporate animations, micro interactions, and subtle visual cues that provide a sense of delight, making the experience more enjoyable and memorable.
- **Accessibility:** Ensure that the design is accessible to users with disabilities. Follow accessibility guidelines and standards to provide inclusive experiences for all users, including those with visual, hearing, or motor impairments.
- **Iterative Design and Testing:** Embrace an iterative design process that involves continuous testing and refinement. Prototype designs, gather feedback from users, and make iterative improvements to the interaction design based on the insights gained.
- **Emotional Connection:** Strive to create an emotional connection between the user and the design. Use visual aesthetics, storytelling, and brand elements to evoke positive emotions and create a memorable experience.
- **Continuous Learning:** Stay updated with the latest trends, technologies, and user behaviors in interactive design. Continuously learn and adapt to evolving user needs and preferences to create innovative and relevant experiences.

References

EEI Jorhat (2022). ICT hand out. http://www.eei-ner.org/wp-content/uploads/2019/09/ICT-Handout.pdf.

Food and Agriculture Organization. (2022). Digital Agriculture. https://www.fao.org/digital-agriculture/en.

https://byjus.com/free-ias-prep/significance-of-e-governance.

MANAGE (2023). Information and communication technology. https://www.manage.gov.in/pgdaem/studymaterial.asp.

MANAGE. (2017). Social media for agricultural extension. https://www.manage.gov.in/publications/extnnext/March2017.pdf.

Raghavendra, C. (2022). Comprehensive and competitive extension. Jaya publishing house.

Ravi G, Amitha Ch. D. and Manasa K. (2022). ICT Enabled Agriculture in India: A Case of Agri Apps: Technology development in agricultural extension. ISBN: 978-93-5570-276-0.

Sagar Mondal. (2018). Textbook of agricultural extension with global innovations. Kalyani Publishers.

Sarvanan, R. (2010). ICT for global extension. New India Publishing Agency.

Shashi Dahiya, Seema Jaggi, K.K. Chaturvedi, Anshu Bhardwaj, R.C Goyal and Cini Varghese. (2012). An eLearning System for Agricultural Education. Indian Res. J. Ext. Edu. 12 (3):132-136.

Vijay Kannade. (2022). Human-computer interaction (HCI) targets the design and implementation of interactive technology. /www.spiceworks.com/tech/artificial-intelligence/articles/what-is-hci/.